From Award-Winning Journalist and Producer

TOM TEICHOLZ

The Third Installment of the **TOMMYWOOD** Series,
a Collection of Columns and Writing on Arts and Culture

For Amy and Natasha

CONTENTS

INTRODUCTION

TOMMYWOOD III, which covers the period from March 2007 through the end of May 2008, contains many columns that I hold particularly dear. I will always be grateful to my editor, Susan Freudenheim, who suggested I write about my father for a Father's Day piece and who let me follow my instinct that there was more to the story than met the eye in the copy of the Nuremberg Laws displayed at the Skirball Cultural Center (subsequent to my article, the Huntington allowed the National Archives in Washington D.C. to take custody of the document).

In this volume, I got to share a meal with Jonathan Gold and hear him utter what may my favorite phrase from a profile, "The plov is great." I also got a chance to interview such cultural landmarks as Mark Rydell, Julius Schulman and William Shatner. I found a way to have Elvis visit the column, take my readers to New Orleans (again), to pay proper tribute to Zsa Zsa Gabor, to mourn the passing of Dutton's bookstore, and to express myself more deeply and at greater length than I had ever before about the genesis of early Bob Dylan.

For all this and more, I thank Rob Eshman, the editor of the *Jewish Journal of Los Angeles* whose continued belief in the importance of Tommywood has allowed the column to flourish. I also want to thank the publicity and press persons, as well as the good friends, who provided access and suggested stories that turned out to better stories than I could have conceived.

Surveying these columns it is worth repeating a remark I have often made that these columns are what paid me the least and yet, made my life the richest. If they did not provide a living, they provide a life.

It's good to be Tommywood.

FOODIE-ISM

This time of year finds me on the treadmill in the mornings, futzing around the gym, taking walks around the neighborhood, eating lots of grilled chicken salads. I'm in training—not for the recent Los Angeles Marathon, but for the marathon weekend in May when my wife and I travel to another city with several like-minded couples without our kids to spend time listening to music and eating, eating, eating. New Orleans is a favorite destination; this year, for a change, we are headed to Vegas.

The research begins months before: Where to eat, what dishes to order, what's new, what's worth revisiting. Can we sneak one more meal in between lunch and dinner? A palate-cleanser? We savor every bite, from the food stands and lunch joints to the fancy and not-so-fancy dinners. I know you're thinking: "That's not healthy!" But it sure is fun.

I may practice Judaism, but I observe Foodie-ism. And Foodie-ism is becoming less and less fun.

Food has become the obsession of an increasingly judgmental nation: We care not just about what we should eat, but what we shouldn't. Adherents of this cult believe that certain foods are inherently good, and others bad. The food police are everywhere, and the political correctness surrounding food has become a topic in recent books from Eric Schlosser's *Fast Food Nation* (Harper Perennial, 2005) to Michael Pollan's *The Omnivore's Dilemma: A Natural History of Four Meals* (Penguin Press, 2006). Foodies appreciate restaurants and chefs much like they once did books or films, and the topic of food now finds its way into discussions of health, medicine, science and travel—it is all-encompassing.

Within this cult, social status rises and falls on where you shop for your food, how it is prepared and where you and your children eat it.

In his new book, *The Gospel of Food* (Ecco/HarperCollins, $25.95), USC sociology professor Barry Glassner discusses how, in his words, we have created "a religion of eating."

Consider the following: Will eating egg yolks shorten our life? Will drinking pomegranate juice extend it? What makes a restaurant exceptional? When is a cuisine "authentic" and does it matter? What is organic? How is it different from "natural"? Is organic or natural produce fresher, healthier, better? Or is it just more expensive?

Increasingly, we define who we are by where and what we eat.

I have often wondered why I am supposed to be impressed when a friend brags that his toddler enjoys sushi (after all, it's not so unusual in Japan). And I have seen the look of horror on a parent's face when she learns that her child loves McDonald's (particularly if the child went there with the nanny). Is fast food really evil?

Don't pretend that you don't have an opinion. But what you think may not be true. Glassner's book is here to tell us that "everything you think you know about food is wrong."

Recently, over an excellent meal downtown at Zucca Ristorante, which I confess included a shared mushroom pizza, Glassner explained that, "pretty much every prescription of how to eat has huge holes in it."

By eating foods with little taste (such as a boneless, skinless chicken breast with no sauce) are we actually extending our lives, and if so by how much? No one can give an exact number. Are we eating foods that we believe are "good" for us, at the cost of actually enjoying what we eat? On the contrary, Glassner quotes many studies that demonstrate that we absorb more nutrients when we enjoy what we eat.

As Glassner makes clear, the science behind many of these studies is imperfect.

No one food or diet suits every person, just as no study can take into account each subject's genetic history, the way their body absorbs nutrients, their stress and the impact of physical activity in their life. They are just postcards of what we, as a society, are choosing to believe at the moment. It is exactly the kind of topic Glassner loves to explore.

Glassner was born in Roanoke, West Virginia, which has a small but tight-knit Jewish community. He attended Northwestern University, graduating with a double major in journalism and sociology, and then received his doctorate in sociology from Washington University in St. Louis. He worked as a journalist for ABC Radio and freelanced for newspapers before returning to academia.

Currently Glassner holds the position of executive vice provost at USC, and he spent six years as the director of the Casden Institute for the study of the Jewish Role in American Life (disclosure: in 2001 Glassner hired me to coauthor the institute's first survey).

Glassner is probably best known for appearing in Michael Moore's *Bowling for Columbine* as the voice of reason speaking about *The Culture of Fear,* his last book in which, as Entertainment Weekly put it "Glassner lucidly exposes how the media and politicians play to Americans' fears, presenting anomalous incidents as rampant dangers."

He has brought the same approach to the subject of food. Glassner focuses a critical eye on the scientific studies that have sought to demonize foods such as the egg yolk, the potato, cheese or whole milk, and he debunks the doctors, nutritionists and writers who promote what he calls "the gospel of naught—the view that the worth of a meal lies principally in what it lacks. The less sugar, salt, fat, calories, carbohydrates, preservatives, additives or other suspect stuff, the better the meal."

His conclusion is that "no food is inherently good or bad." Much like the scene in Woody Allen's *Sleeper,* we have learned that foods that were thought to be "bad," like chocolate, coffee or wine, have now been found to have health benefits.

Over the course of five years spent on the book, Glassner had some amazing meals, he told me, at some of the country's best restaurants, such as The French Laundry in Napa Valley, Daniel in New York and Spago in Beverly Hills. *The Gospel of Food* explains what makes these restaurants and their chefs great, and also why the reviewers tend to have great meals there (generally the restaurants know who they are and give them better meals). He also enjoyed a great variety of ethnic cuisines, becoming familiar with the varieties of Thai cuisine, Korean cooking and even a Korean version of Chinese food.

As part of his research, Glassner also talked to food chemists, nutritionists, and business executives in the food industry.

In his book Glassner shares with us the surprises he encountered along the way, such as the great chefs working for McDonalds and Burger King; or how natural foods can include "natural" filler, such as wood pulp, and can be more processed than foods that do not carry that label. Similarly, Glassner recounts how Americans spend $2 billion a year on food with added vitamins, minerals or herbs that provide no proven health benefit and may interfere with prescribed drugs.

"I'm interested in where these ideas come from," Glassner said. "Who benefits from them?"

Would you be shocked, shocked, shocked to learn that the beneficiaries are politicians, advocacy groups, agri-business and product marketers—each of whom has a large stake in having us behave in a particular way? Glassner details how each profits from a shift in dietary attitudes. Make no mistake: Billions of dollars are at stake in getting us to eat certain products.

Glassner also devotes a chapter to McDonald's and fast food restaurants, which, as the K-Fed Super Bowl ad indicates, are routinely mocked and blamed for everything from obesity to the breakdown of family values. Glassner makes a compelling argument for the value inherent in "value meals" for the poor, the harried, the homeless. And we all know how good the French fries are.

Which brings us to Glassner's final chapter and the question on all our minds: "What made America fat?"

Glassner asks some good questions: In the fifties, sixties and seventies, the average diet consisted of all the bad foods that we are told not to eat today. (I can still recall the oil sizzling as my mother placed the veal cutlets, soaked in egg and milk and covered in breadcrumbs, in the cast-iron skillet to make my favorite meal of wienerschnitzel). Yet there was no epidemic of obesity. So what changed?

It's not fast food. Glassner shows that the proliferation of fast food establishments preceded the obesity epidemic by a decade.

Glassner suggests one important difference: People smoke less. According to studies cited by Glassner, during the period obesity rates shot up (the 1980s-1990s), the number of smokers declined by a third—and former smokers on average gain ten to twenty pounds after quitting. So this may account for some of the national weight gain. Conversely, is it also possible that people stopping smoking is the reason for a decrease in heart disease (as much or more so than eating low fat foods)?

But what about childhood obesity, you may ask.

I asked Glassner this very question. "No question there are more sugary drinks and candies," he said. But the question remains: "What has dramatically changed?" Glassner believes that one big change is that kids today enjoy "a lot less physical activity." One reason for this harkens back to Glassner's last book, *The Culture of Fear.*

"Parents are afraid of letting children out of their sight," he said. Decades ago children spent their free time outside playing and exploring. Today overprotective parents are afraid to let their children play by themselves outdoors for fear they will be abducted or be put in harm's way.

Finally, Glassner suggests the possibility that for both adults and children, our culture of diets and diet foods may be responsible. Any diet that restricts certain foods that our body (or our psyche) craves may cause us to binge on them and other foods. Could years of yo-yoing from fad diet to fad diet have resulted in the increase in obesity? As a group of Harvard and Stanford scientists put it: Dieting to control weight is not only ineffective, it may actually promote weight gain. I certainly can believe that.

In my own lifetime, I can recall attempting the Royal Canadian Air Force Diet, the Scarsdale Diet, Atkins, The Zone and the South Beach Diet. I have watched national crazes over grapefruit diets, cabbage diets, even ice cream diets. I have seen waves of food pronouncements on red meat, carbohydrates, dairy products, grains, pastas and fruits and vegetables.

Over the years, I have lost hundreds of pounds—actually, the same twenty to thirty pounds over and over again. Although rationally I realize that my body is genetically programmed to give me the winning physique of my Eastern European forebears who were short and stout of bearing, I still cling to the notion that there is a better-idealized version of myself to achieve (the only difference being that the weight at which I once began my diet is now the weight that I strive to reach). But given the positive effects of statins on lowering cholesterol, is yo-yo dieting more dangerous than enjoying the foods you like? Where does this leave us?

I am reminded of the old joke about the tenor Luciano Pavarotti, whose doctor tells him to go on a diet. He goes to his favorite trattoria and asks his favorite waiter: "Tell me which is the healthiest sandwich for me to order?"

To which the waiter answers: "Maestro, for you, the healthiest sandwich is…half a sandwich."

Perhaps it is best to focus on fit, not fat. Although Glassner's book provides no prescription for a healthy diet, when pressed, Glassner answered that in matters of food, "Turns out your mother was right." (I assure you he is referring to his mother, not mine—mine was getting injections of sheep's urine to lose weight and buttering my bread with cream cheese.)

His recommendation: "Enjoy what you eat; eat moderately, eat your fruits and vegetables."

Or to sum it up in two words: "Eat well."

Good advice that I intend to follow and would like to discuss further, but I have some meals to plan for my Foodie-ism holiday.

March 15, 2007

A TREASURE TROVE

THE MILKEN ARCHIVE OF JEWISH MUSIC

Can you tell the story of a people by its music? Last November, the classical music label Naxos released the fiftieth CD of its *American Classics* series, music from the Milken Archive of American Jewish Music, so the time has come to give the archive its props (just imagine Randy Jackson saying: Yo! Yo! Dog, check it out...).

The Milken Archive defines American Jewish Music as "music inspired by or relating to the American Jewish experience." The Naxos recordings cover a vast range of music, secular and religious, from Leonard Bernstein's early Jewish music to "Kaddish," from "Great Songs of the American Yiddish Stage" to Ladino love songs and chants and prayers from the Colonial era.

Music that, in many instances, had never been recorded. You need neither to be Jewish to love these Jewish recordings nor even to be Jewish to be included in the archives—the archive has recorded Thomas Beveridge's ecumenical "Yizkor Requiem" and Dave Brubeck's "The Gates of Justice," a cantata based on Jewish biblical texts and African American spirituals.

What is comparable to the accomplishment of this archive? It is a bit like Alan Lomax's project to record American folk music for the Library of Congress. Lomax's wide-ranging recordings not only captured a slice of American life, they also preserved a whole treasure trove of American culture and gave recognition to artists few had ever heard or otherwise would ever have known. The recordings of what has come to be called "American Roots Music" (from Woody Guthrie to Muddy Waters) inspired a generation of singer-songwriters who, in turn, have inspired successive generations to this day. The achievement of the Milken Archive is no less grand and its global impact may, with time, be just as great.

Recently, I dropped by the offices of the Milken Family Foundation to chat with Richard Sandler about the archive and to learn its history and discuss its future. Sandler is the executive vice president of the Milken Foundation and a partner in the law firm of Maron & Sandler; he has been involved in the foundation and the archive since its inception.

As he explained, businessman and philanthropist Lowell Milken, co-founder and chairman of the Milken Family Foundation, had a long-standing interest in American Jewish Music—he even commissioned a piece from Michael Isaacson for one of his children's b'nai mitzvah. Milken has written that conversations with American Jewish composers during the 1980s led him to believe that a "collective memory" of Jewish music would be lost if not collected and recorded.

Around 1990, he conceived the idea of an archive of American Jewish music, an idea that took wing as Neil W. Levin, formerly of the Jewish Theological Seminary, joined the archive as musical director in 1993.

"We came up with this idea that if we are going to do this on a first-class basis with world-class musicians, there is an advantage to recording in Europe." Sandler explained. European orchestras, which are subsidized by their governments, were looking for new repertoires to record and would do so at reasonable rates.

As a result, although the archive did record with the Seattle Symphony in this country, they also recorded in Barcelona, Berlin, Prague, Vienna and London, with the added benefit that the music was played (and in some cases, broadcast on radio) all over Europe.

According to the Milken Archive's own publication, they have recorded "700 pieces, more than 100 CDs [worth of music], representing the work of more than 200 composers, many of which are world premiere recordings."

But having recorded the music, they now had to decide how best to distribute it. They considered producing their own CDs, or distributing the musically digitally. Instead, the archive's Paul Schwendener, who holds the titles of chief operating officer, director of marketing and artist and repertoire adviser, introduced the Milken Archive to Naxos, a classical musical label with worldwide distribution, which was "fascinated by the project."

Naxos is known for producing reasonably priced CDs that make the classical repertoire accessible. For Naxos, the fact that the material was already recorded was attractive; for the archive it was compelling that Naxos showed tremendous interest at a time when other labels were cutting back. It was, according to Sandler, "a perfect fit." Naxos agreed to produce fifty CDs over a three-year period.

The results have been impressive: Naxos has sold more than 200,000 CDs of the Jewish American Music Archive recordings worldwide, in more than fifty-seven countries, with sales split equally between North America and abroad.

Among the most popular are recordings of Kurt Weill's *The Eternal Road,* a work that was first performed in 1937 with a cast of more than 300 and speaks to the dream of a Zionist homeland; *Great Songs From the Yiddish Theater,* featuring works by Abraham Ellstein and members of his circle, and the aforementioned "Gates of Justice" by Brubeck. However, what's even more surprising has been the strong sales of some of the more religious and esoteric material, such as a Sephardic service, a collection of cantorial favorites and a recording of a High Holiday service.

Among the archive's greatest discoveries was Jewish music by celebrated French composer Darius Milhaud. Sandler describes his "Service Sacré" as "a real jewel." The archive also was able to reconstruct "The Genesis Suite," a collaboration between several European exile composers, such as Stravinsky, Schoenberg and Toch—who were working in Hollywood and whose score was thought lost—that had only been performed once in 1945 at the Hollywood Bowl after World War II.

Music, however, is only one part of the accomplishment. Over the years, the Milken Archive has also videotaped more than 800 hours of interviews with such important figures as Robert Merrill, Jan Peerce, Hugo Weisgall, and Ralph Shapey. It has also recorded interviews with prominent cantors; stars of the Yiddish musical theater, such as Seymour Rechzeit, who recalled the history of the theater, and some of his fellow performers, such as Molly Picon.

Among the most memorable is an interview with Herman Berlinski. German-born Berlinski, who fled his homeland in the 1930s, returned in 2000 to oversee the recording of his Avodat Shabbat prayer service in Berlin performed by a German orchestra. "He never imagined [such a thing would occur]" Sandler recalls. "It made his entire life worthwhile." So what's next for the Milken Archive? It has a variety of projects under consideration. Although Naxos has released fifty CDs, the Milken Archive is considering offering a complete set of its recordings to institutions in hard form (CDs) or digitally; making a documentary based on the oral histories; creating a permanent or traveling exhibition on American Jewish music; and/or developing a curriculum—using American Jewish music as a way to study American Jewish cultural history.

"One of our goals is to figure out the best way to make the music available to the people who want to perform it. Not every concert of our archive needs to be performed by us. The goal is access to as many people as possible."

Sandler says he finds great satisfaction knowing that "what Lowell conceived of will be here 100 years from now. It will be here, and it wouldn't be here if we hadn't done it."

I asked Sandler whether through his work at the archive he had uncovered a special connection between music and the Jewish People. Sandler admitted that he had thought a lot about it, but had come to no definitive answer. However, it had crossed his mind that "as a nomadic people, one of the things that's very easy to take with you is your music."

The history of Jews in America is but 350 years old—yet there exists a wealth of music, striking in its breadth and diversity, that tells a story that ranges from the prayer rooms to theater stages and the concert halls, that is secular and spiritual, comic and majestic, speaking of history and private life. It is complemented by a record of the people who created and performed that music that is now available, thanks to the Milken Archive, to be heard, studied, played and enjoyed. You may even ignore it—safe in the knowledge that it is there for you to discover tomorrow and there for the generations that follow.

As jazz legend Charlie Parker once said, "Music is your own experience, your thoughts, your wisdom."

Now, the Milken Archive is our own.

March 29, 2007

REBEL WITH A CAUSE

Andrew Stevens, a longtime Beverly Hills resident, successful businessman, active philanthropist and Hungarian Holocaust survivor, is hard to resist. He's in his late seventies but looks fifteen years younger—not because of his hair, which is darker than nature permits, but because of his energy, drive and determination. He has a quality I find hard to describe (but which many, who have had occasion to befriend Holocaust survivors, will recognize) that is annoying yet endearing.

Let me explain: In the course of reporting this column, before I had even had a chance to contact him, he called to ask me why I hadn't called him yet. Over the next week or so, he called me on my cellphone. He called me at home on the weekend. He invited me to his office.

He faxed me articles about him. He gave me copies of a speech he'd delivered. He invited me to lunch. He wanted me to tell him "the angle" of this article. He asked if he could see the article before I turned it in to my editors. (I said no.) He also gave me a copy and asked me to mention a book of poems called, *Shoah Never Again* (Jim White Enterprises), written (and self-published) by his friend, James E. White Jr., an African American writer and television producer (OK, now I've mentioned it).

And the day the column was due, he called again to say he had "one more input" for me. And he asked again to see the column before I turned it in. (I said no again.)

So why write a column about Stevens? In spite of this barrage, the more time I spent with him, the more compelled I was by the charisma of Stevens and the more I wanted to tell his story.

The ostensible reason for this column is the recently published *Brothers for Resistance and Rescue: The Underground Zionist Youth Movement in Hungary During World War II,* by David Gur (Gefen Publishing House), in which Stevens appears.

Brothers for Resistance is an important contribution to understanding the Holocaust in Hungary and the resistance work carried out by so many young men and women. As the foreword notes, Gur, who was himself active in the underground, spent two decades trying to track down as many comrades and fellow resistance members as possible for this work.

The book explains the various political, religious and social factions that operated as part of the resistance. Many are still active in various political groups in present-day Israel, such as Mapai (Labor), Dror Habonim (Zionist-Socialist), Mizrahi (Religious Zionism) and Beitar (Activist Zionist). Gur gives the history of these groups and more.

The book explores the many diverse activities of the underground that Zionist youth groups undertook to save as many lives as possible during the Holocaust. These included sending emissaries to towns and cities to warn and prepare them, smuggling people out of Hungary to safer havens (this mission was called the "tiyul"), the production of forged documents, as well as the building of armed bunkers for hiding people.

He also tells of how children were taken to houses under the protection of the Red Cross, and adults and children brought to buildings that were under the protection of foreign legations. In the course of underground activity, young men posing in uniform risked their lives to free others from labor camps and prisons.

However, the biographical entries are the heart and the soul of the book. As Gur said in the foreword, "The motivation behind the work was the wish to rescue underground activists from all streams from anonymity and to reveal their actions."

More than 400 men and women are listed, each one a chronicle of heroism.

Gur's entry on Stevens reveals that he was born Endre Steinberger and was just sixteen when the Nazis occupied Budapest in 1944. Conscripted into forced labor, he escaped. After receiving forged documents from a friend, he became involved in the manufacture of documents.

Stevens worked out of several apartments in Budapest. However, early one morning, the Hungarian fascist police, the Arrow Cross, knocked on his door and apprehended him. As he was led down the street to prison and certain death, he ran away. They shot at him, and despite taking a bullet to his ankle, he escaped.

Stevens returned to the manufacture of forged documents. Stevens recalled to me that there was a deaf-mute man who worked beside him who, with a penknife, was able to cut rubber stamps to resemble official seals. Stevens' task was filing out forged documents, and he also often delivered and distributed them, saving many lives, including Laszlo Weinberger, one of his schoolmates.

Stevens recalled that on one occasion, Raoul Wallenberg, the Swedish diplomat who handed out Swedish papers to Jews, saving their lives, complained that he had run out of official forms to fill out. Otto Komoly, one of the Hungarian resistance leaders, offered to provide Wallenberg with a stack of forged forms. Wallenberg agreed, and Stevens delivered them to his office.

Stevens' false papers were also instrumental in saving his mother's life after she escaped from a death march and hid until war's end.

For his actions during the war, Stevens received the Golden Cross from Hungarian President Apad Gonz in 1997, following which Rep. Tom Lantos (D-San Mateo), who is also a Hungarian Holocaust survivor, paid tribute to Stevens in the Congressional Record.

Looking back, Stevens says, he feels those ten months when he worked in the Hungarian resistance are his "proudest moments."

He is not just proud that he survived, he told me, but that in a time of crisis, he helped others. "I could have just kept my false papers and sat in a room. Today, I can't even understand how I could do that."

He was constantly in danger: "Every hour, you could be next."

The false papers only provided minor protection.

"If I was caught, all they needed to do [to find out if I was a Jew] was to ask me pull down my pants," he said.

Yet he traveled all over Budapest without fear.

Stevens still can't understand how so many of his fellow Hungarian Jews remained blind to the fact of what was happening. "In the beginning, we didn't believe...but at a certain point...by then it was too late."

Stevens recalled how he personally witnessed the murder of many Hungarian Jews by the banks of the Danube.

"With my own eyes, I saw little kids laughing and then [the soldiers] tossing them into the air and shooting at them," he said.

Today at the base of the Margit Bridge in Budapest there is a memorial—little bronze shoes stuck in the mud. (Documentary filmmaker Bela Mayer just sent me a short film by Andras Salamon on this subject called, *Tell Your Children* at films.thelot.com/films/17451).

In 1949, Stevens immigrated to the United States, eventually traveling to California. His first job here was as a busboy at Mama Weiss, a Hungarian restaurant that used to exist in Beverly Hills. He worked as a waiter's assistant at the Cock 'n' Bull on Sunset, pumped gas and worked in a lighting factory. Eventually he became a real estate sales agent, selling graded land for residential development in the east San Gabriel Valley.

Over time, he fielded a team of sales agents who handled large home sites in Big Bear, Montebello, the Salton Riviera and Thousand Palms. Stevens was also instrumental in the development of Lake Havasu, Ariz. His company grew to develop, market and manage properties not only in the United States but also abroad, including Brussels, Hong Kong, Guam and even Budapest.

Stevens has two grown sons, a doctor and a lawyer, from his first marriage, and a seven-year-old son from his second marriage.

His charitable activities are legion (Stevens suggested I refer to him as "Rebel With a Cause," which he informed me was his trademark), and include ORT, Vista Del Mar, the Beverly Hills Rotary Club, DARE, The Medallions (Cedar-Sinai Medical Center's fundraising division), Ben-Gurion University of the Negev and the Emanuel Foundation, a charitable organization devoted to restoring and preserving sites of Jewish interest in Hungary, named in honor of Emanuel Schwartz, Tony Curtis' father (Curtis provided the original seed money).

My mother was active in the Emmanuel Foundation, and many years ago, after I first moved to Los Angeles, she asked me to serve as the LA driver/assistant/factotum for the foundation's executive director, Andor Weiss, a Brooklyn-based Orthodox rabbi and Hungarian survivor.

"You're my Hollywood connection," he used to say to me, to which I would reply: "If I'm your Hollywood connection, then you are in trouble."

The rabbi was about four feet tall, bald, smart as a fox and tenacious as a terrier. Whenever he was in town, I had no idea where our adventures would take us, but thanks to him, I found myself in a limo with Guy McElwayne, hearing stories about Frank Sinatra and his daughter, Tina; and schmoozing at the home of Joe Esterzhas in Malibu. And on one memorable occasion, I was greeted at the door of a condo in Bel Air by a bare-chested Tony Curtis, who proceeded to hug me.

The West Coast director of the Emanuel Foundation? Stevens. So, in fact, I knew Stevens, having met him several times a decade ago. But I did not know his story—and I did not really know him.

This Sunday, April 15, Yom HaShoah (Holocaust Remembrance Day) will be observed in Pan Pacific Park at the Holocaust Memorial. Stevens will be there in a place of honor. As a survivor, as a member of the resistance, as one of the supporters of the memorial, he deserves it.

To return to my original question: Why write a column about Stevens?

That same spirit that made him run away when arrested by the Arrow Cross and kept him running even when shot; that made him save others, even when his own life was at risk is the same headstrong independent personality that forged a business and a life in this country, and that continues to be charitable. He doesn't stop. He doesn't say no; so who can say no to him?

At the outset of this column, I said Stevens was annoying. Perhaps I should have said insistent. But I can tell you this: My parents, Eastern European Holocaust survivors, were also each, in their own way, very charming but on occasion extremely annoying people. It was hard to say no to them. So you could say the reason I wrote this column is simple: I miss them.

April 12, 2007

THE NEXT (BOOK) CONVERSATION

Can a conversation inspire a city? A people?
Nextbook, an organization devoted to Jewish literature, culture and ideas (www.nextbook.org) came to LA last weekend, staging a full day festival at UCLA's MacGowan and Freud theaters called "Acting Jewish: Film, TV, Comedy, Music," the first of what it hopes to be an annual event.

According to Nextbook Director Julie Sandorf, the notion of an LA festival was inspired by Pulitzer Prize-winning playwright, filmmaker and author David Mamet, whose book, *The Wicked Son,* Nextbook published with Shocken. The festival's purpose, Nextbook Program Director Matthew Brogan declared, was to bring "together writers, actors, directors, and musicians to talk about the imaginary Jews of popular culture and their real life counterparts."

Mamet agreed to participate in the event, in a conversation on the subject of "Make Believe Jews," in the words of the event's program, "about how Hollywood has treated the Jews and his own attempts to create a different kind of onscreen Jewish character."

Mamet's interlocutor was none other than yours truly. I must now disclose that I was paid an honorarium for the pleasure and the challenge of doing so (they actually handed me a check when I walked off stage!); and that for the occasion I purchased a new jacket at Sean, my favorite men's store (I didn't need to disclose that part; I just wanted to). Sandorf introduced me as "a great friend of Nextbook," which is a compliment I accept. Such is my bias to take into account as I share my subjective impressions of the event.

On Saturday evening, Los Angeles Times film critic Kenneth Turan hosted a screening of two silent films. First was D. W. Griffith's 1910 short *A Child of the Ghetto,* which featured footage shot on New York's Lower East Side. It was akin to traveling in a time machine to see the bustling activity of families and street peddlers on Rivington Street (today's equivalent would be walking down Alvarado Street in Los Angeles toward Langer's Deli, where the vibrant ethnic community is Latin rather than Eastern European Jews); followed by *East and West,* a 1923 Yiddish film starring a young Molly Picon that established the pixy-ish qualities that would, in a few years, make Picon the highest paid Yiddish actress in the world.

Sunday, Nextbook presented eight different panels on film, TV, Hollywood novels, food, and music including such diverse presenters and topics as Bruce Jay Friedman, Bruce Wagner and Ella Taylor on the Hollywood novel; Frank London, Jewlia Eisenberg and Josh Kun talking Jewish music; and Jonahan Gold, Leslie Brenner, Evan Kleiman and Jeffrey Shandler discussing food and film. The panels overlapped and intersected and, like any festival, there was always the risk that you were missing something interesting happening somewhere else.

For example, while I was on stage with Mamet, Turan was in another hall sharing the exuberant ethnically Jewish pre-code film comedies of Max Davidson—a presentation I would have been eager to attend. Similarly, I missed seeing my friend, journalist David Margolick, participate in the panel on "Jewish Stardom," which also included USC professor Leo Braudy (one of the most knowledgeable film experts around); artist, essayist and self-proclaimed Jew-ologist Rhonda Lieberman; and the very learned and entertaining Jeffrey Shandler, who co-authored with Jim Hoberman the excellent and essential *Entertaining America: Jews, Movies and Broadcasting*—all because I rushed to hear Adam Gopnik talk about Jewish comedy.

Gopnik was, much like his essays in the New Yorker, erudite, charming and polished. He revealed that he arrived in New York in 1979 hoping to be a stand-up comic, or a songwriter—and it is safe to say that he has become a literary tummler, heir to a tradition of reporting and performance, part Robert Benchley, part Calvin Trillin. As for my conversation with David Mamet, I have little recollection of what was said (my mind always goes blank the minute I leave the stage), but I've been told a podcast will be available soon from Nextbook.

My friends and family report that the conversation covered a full spectrum of Jews on film, from Mamet's own childhood performances for the Chicago Board of Rabbis, to the Yiddish Theater in Odessa, the Group Theater in New York, *The Jazz Singer, Exodus,* movies about the Holocaust, and Jewish characters Mamet has created, including a recent episode of "The Unit" called "Two Coins" that took place in Israel.

I've been told that often the most important information in a psychoanalytic session is revealed in the last few minutes, just as we often put the most important info into the P.S. of a communication. One of the highlights of Mamet's appearance for me came in a follow-up question from the audience when Mamet told, or more correctly in the parlance of Hollywood, pitched the assembled listeners a story involving both an Israeli fighter pilot and tales from Rabbi Isaac Luria that he hopes to write and direct.

But that was just my panel. I spent the rest of the day bouncing among the presentations. Here are some things that struck me:

• Nextbook's Sara Ivry hosted a panel of young actors whom she ably cajoled into some trenchant revelations. Actor Adam Goldberg (*Saving Private Ryan*), whose mother is not Jewish, related it wasn't until he was auditioning for film roles in LA that he found himself being typecast for Jewish parts, while being told he's "too Jewish" for other parts. By contrast, in TV, Goldberg explained, he is rarely cast as someone identified as a "Jew." Laura Silverman, who plays Sarah Silverman's sister on her TV program (and is her sister), said that she often goes up for Jewish parts, which are then awarded to actresses of Latin or Italian heritage, but when she goes up for parts that are Italian or non-Jewish, she is always dismissed as "Jewish." Both actors said they believe parts should be cast free from any ethnic consideration—but wish they also got the benefit of such "blind" casting. Both said they had, at one point, considered changing their names.

• Meital Dohan, an Israeli-born actress who appears in *Weeds* as Yael Hoffman, said that most casting directors thought her name "exotic" rather than Hebrew and wanted to cast her as Russian more than Jewish.

• In his presentation, Adam Gopnik traced three generations of humor from Henny Youngman (his grandfather's era) to Woody Allen (his father's time) to Seinfeld (his own era). But he felt that he had reached a point where he could understand the humor of, but not always laugh at, the outrageous comedy his children enjoy from such current performers as Sarah Silverman and Sascha Baron Cohen (which is the way I feel about such animated fare as *The Simpsons, South Park* and *Family Guy*—I get what's funny, it even makes me laugh sometimes, but as humor it's just not for me).

• Bruce Jay Friedman revealed that the older he gets, the more Jewish he has become. He explained that when he was younger and wrote his novels and stories, such as "The Heartbreak Kid," although audiences thought of them as Jewish, he viewed them as about characters caught in predicaments.

• Bruce Wagner was funny, intelligent, perceptive, deep and heartfelt—reminding me that whenever I hear Wagner speak, I am always struck by the fact that this man who at times looks like Max Schreck on a break from shooting Nosferatu and who has written novels filled with toxic levels of anomie, is in person warm, considerate, thoughtful, and passionate about what he is attempting to achieve in his novels.

• Evan Kleinman hosted a panel on food and film with LA Weekly's Jonathan Gold, the just-named Pulitzer Prize winner, Leslie Brenner, food editor of the Los Angeles Times, and Jeffrey Shandler, in which they all pondered why there was no Jewish American film equivalent of foreign films celebrating food such as *Eat Man, Drink, Woman, Like Water for Chocolate* or even *La Grande Bouffe*. Good question—with no definitive answer except to say that the Jewish experience of food is connected to guilt, family and sex. Accordingly, they screened memorable dinner scenes from films and TV programs such as *Annie Hall* and *Sex and the City*.

• Finally, hipsters Frank London of Klezmatics fame, Jewlia Eisenberg (yes—that's how she spells her first name) of Charming Hostess and Josh Kun, whom you may know from the recent *Jewface* CD and who has recently joined the faculty of USC's Annenberg School for Communication, at one point took their audience on a musical journey through time and space, playing music by Jewish artists from all over the Levant and explaining the specific meaning of certain notes and scales in a manner that made you realize the sacred and hypnotic power of music.

The day after the event, questions popped into my head: Was the conference too academic or intellectual? A case of too many panelists talking about movies, music and books, rather than seeing (or listening to) writers and artists performing their work? Was the audience, the majority of whom were over forty, too old? What does it take to get people thirty and under to attend? How many attendees does it take to make a festival successful? Worth repeating? Does Los Angeles need a festival of Jewish culture? What does it accomplish?

I know the questions are worth asking, but I'm not sure the answers matter. Particularly given that the traditional Jewish answer to the question, "Does it help?" is: "It doesn't hurt."

What impressed me, overall, is how collegial the event was. There were near 500 attendees throughout the course of the day, and people fell into conversation with each other, as if shared interests were introduction enough. This held true for presenters as well as audience members. Lunch was available on the courtyard in front of the theaters and in the Murphy Sculpture Garden, and as a klezmer band played, a large crowd of people, many of whom did not know each other, sat down in various groupings together, and each joined in their own conversations.

It was, to this observer, a rare moment—one that doesn't happen in Los Angeles enough.

LA is a city of kindred souls waiting to find each other. To the extent that Nextbook can stage an event that gets people to engage, to be entertained, to learn about Jewish artists, writers, musicians, performers and movies they never knew about, or to revisit or reconsider them—they are fulfilling their mission. The conversations they inspire can bind us, sustain us, fulfill us; but most important, they create a hunger for more, for the next conversation.

April 26, 2007

WHOSE NUREMBERG LAWS ARE
THEY ANYWAY?

Sometimes we take for granted what is right in front of us.
Consider that one of the most important documents of
the twentieth century is right here in Los Angeles, accessible and on view for all to visit. Few realize it; fewer still appreciate it.

Although originals of the Declaration of Independence, the
Constitution and the Bill of Rights can be found at the National
Archives in Washington, and the Magna Carta and the Rosetta
Stone are part of the collection of the British Library in London,
how many people know that there is an original typescript of
the infamous Nuremberg Laws, signed by Adolf Hitler, Wilhem
Frick (minister of the interior), Franz Gurtner (minister of justice) and Rudolf Hess (Hitler's deputy) on display here in Los
Angeles at the Skirball Cultural Center and Museum. I've been
to the Skirball on many occasions, but how many times have I
walked by the case and not paid attention to its contents?

How the Nuremberg Laws came to California in the possession of Gen. George S. Patton, who left them to reside first
at the Huntington Museum and Library in Pasadena and now

at the Skirball, is a story explored in the recently released book, *Bloodlines: Recovering Hitler's Nuremberg Laws From Patton's Trophy to Public Memorial* by Anthony M. Platt and Cecilia E. O'Leary" (Paradigm).

Platt, a professor emeritus at Cal State Sacramento, and his wife, O'Leary, professor of American history at Cal Sate Monterey Bay, write that "little did we imagine that...[writing this book] would lead us to an exploration of modern European history, Nazi legislation, the relationship between anti-Semitism and racism, fascist sympathies among California's elite and the cultural politics of libraries...and [for Platt] would trigger an exploration of contradictions in my own Jewish identity."

Along the way, they conclude that Patton "looted and violated his own orders" in taking the documents as his own, as Platt recently told me. But as to who has proper claim to the papers, how we should regard the Huntington's role in conserving them (and keeping them secret for a half century), the Skirball's choices in displaying them and why we should care about this typescript of the laws is a larger discussion.

First the facts:

The Nuremberg Laws—so-named because Hitler ordered their passage during the 1935 Nazi Party rally in Nuremberg—consist of three directives:

• The Reich Flag Law made the swastika the national symbol, and at the same time, prohibited Jews from hoisting the flag. It was signed by Hitler, Interior Minister Frick and Gen. Werner von Blomberg, minister of war

• The Citizenship Law prohibited Jews from being German citizens, thereby stripping German Jews of their citizenship in their own country. It was signed by Hitler and Frick.

• The Law for the Protection of German Blood and Honor barred Jews from marrying or having sexual relations with non-Jews. It also prohibited Jews from employing Germans under 45 as servants. It was signed by Hitler, Frick, Justice Minister Gurtner and Hess.

Dated Sept. 15, 1935, these laws were approved unanimously by the Nazi government and printed and distributed throughout Germany the next day.

Almost a decade later, on June 11, 1945, Patton presented an envelope containing the Nuremberg Laws to Huntington trustee Robert Millikan. Patton had grown up in Pasadena, and his father had been a personal friend of Edward Huntington, the library's founder. In depositing the papers, Patton asked that there be no press and that the envelope be safeguarded in the Huntington's vault. Two months earlier, Patton had sent the Huntington a presentation copy of Hitler's *Mein Kampf* inscribed by Patton to the Huntington.

While he was there, Patton dictated a statement describing how he had come into possession of the laws—he explained that in Nuremberg, the troops of the 90th Infantry "found a vault, not opened, and persuaded a German to open it for them. In it they found this thing." Patton went on to explain that the soldiers arranged for Gen. James A. Van Vleet, commander of the ninetieth, to make a public presentation of the laws to Patton. "So it is my property," Patton concluded.

Patton returned to Europe. Six months later, on December 21, 1945, Patton died from injuries received in a car accident.

Fifty-four years after Patton's visit to the library, on June 26, 1999, the Huntington revealed to the world that a rare, original copy of the laws, which had been in their possession since

1945, would soon go on public display—at the Skirball Cultural Center on "indefinite loan." The loan was being made, the Huntington declared, as a gesture of support and friendship to the Skirball, which had opened in its new home in the Sepulveda Pass in 1996. The Skirball revealed the documents in a public display a few days later.

At the time the loan was announced, Huntington president Robert Skotheim said he hoped this loan would be seen as outreach by the Huntington, a traditionally insular institution. "We now feel we have a broader obligation to serve the public," Skotheim told the Christian Science Monitor.

Instead, as Platt recounts, press accounts at the time, most notably by Sharon Waxman (then of the *Washington Post*; today she reports for *The New York Times*) were more interested in why the Huntington kept the documents secret for more than fifty years and why they were never displayed or loaned to other institutions. Skotheim offered several explanations: Patton had asked that they be put in the vault, and they were not released or shared or noted because they did not relate to the Huntington's other collections or to the focus of the research done there. The press reports remained skeptical.

At the time, authors Platt and O'Leary were spending the summer at the library as Huntington fellows, researching California cultural history. They immediately became engaged by the unfolding story and began the study that would eventually become *Bloodlines*. On July 19, a few weeks after the revelation, a letter appeared in the Washington Post written by Martin Dannenberg, disputing Patton's account. Dannenberg, then eighty-three and living in Baltimore, said that as a special agent with the US Army's Counter Intelligence Corps, he and two other agents, Maxwell Pickens of Bessemer, Alabama, and Frank Perls of Los Angeles, had recovered the laws from a bank vault not in Nuremberg but in nearby Eichstatt and had turned them over to Patton's intelligence chief, with the understanding that they would be forwarded to the Allies' intelligence headquarters in Paris, where documents were being collected for war crimes trials. Dannenberg concluded that Patton never sent the documents but "kept them as a personal souvenir that made its way into the Huntington Library."

Dannenberg also wrote a lengthier account to the Skirball itself. At the same time, Platt and O'Leary interviewed Dannenberg, first by phone, then in person, and, in their words, "vetted" his account, concluding in a letter sent to officials at the Skirball, the Huntington and to Waxman at the Washington Post that they believed Dannenberg's account. They also believed it likely that "Patton had knowingly looted an important Nazi document."

Dannenberg later recalled that the laws were found "by two Jewish boys and a Southern Baptist." Pickens had died long ago and little information was available about him. By contrast, Perls, the son of prominent European art dealers, who as Jews were forced to flee Berlin, eventually opened his own celebrated art gallery in Los Angeles with the support of fellow emigre and art collector Billy Wilder. Although Perls died in 1975, his niece was still alive and provided Platt with access to Perls' papers, which supported Dannenberg's account.

The initial Skirball display said that "the typescript was presented to" Patton who, in turn, "donated" it to the Huntington. In September 1999, when the Skirball's main building was being retro-fitted, the laws' display case was dismantled. Moshe

Safdie, architect of the Skirball building, designed a new special case for the Nuremberg Laws, and the Skirball invited Dannenberg and his family to the official unveiling of the new case, which took place on December 12, 1999.

By then, in response to Dannenberg's account and supporting photographs he provided, the informational text inside the case had been changed. Patton's dictated account of how the laws came into his possession had been removed and returned to the Huntington. Also gone was a photo of Patton at the Huntington delivering the envelope containing the laws to trustee Millikan. In its place, was a photo of Dannenberg. The text was also changed. It now read that Patton had "deposited" the typescript rather than donated it.

The Nuremberg Laws continue to stand in Safdie's special wedge-shaped case, as they have since being revealed for the second time. They are still on "indefinite loan" from the Huntington, displayed as part of the Skirball's permanent exhibition, *Vision and Values,* a triumphalist account of the American Jewish encounter.

The display does not focus exclusively on America—it also incorporates both items and elements that Jews from foreign lands brought with them to this country, and it takes detours to include features on the Holocaust and Israel—to illustrate the consciousness of American Jews. The Nuremberg case is called, *Prelude to Catastrophe,* and stands at the entrance to the enclosure that discusses the Holocaust.

In a recent conversation, Robert Kirschner, vice president of special projects at the Skirball, said the museum made the changes to its explanatory label because the Skirball's "only interest is to be accurate." As for the history of the documents, the issues of provenance are "not ours to determine," Kirschner said, "because it is a loan." This opinion is shared by Platt, as well. Given the importance of the signed typescripts and the importance of publicly exhibiting them in a "context of Jewish history and an appreciation of Jewish ideals," Kirschner said, "our point of view is that we are grateful to the Huntington Library."

Platt reserves the brunt of his criticism for the Huntington. Platt's book provides a richly detailed and well-documented account not only of the Nuremberg Laws but of the Huntington itself, its founder and the trustees and officials and their politics and prejudices, and how they informed the institution.

Platt also details Patton's own racism and anti-Semitism. In researching the connections between eugenics in California and racial policies in Germany and between the Huntington family and Patton's, and the history not only of San Marino, where the Huntington resides, but also California itself, Platt reveals not so much a conspiracy as an old boys club of like-minded people.

For Platt, writing about the Huntington and the Nuremberg Laws also became a personal journey. As part of *Bloodlines,* he reflects on his own history as a Jewish child in Northern England and the extent to which he disassociated himself from that background, both as a student at Oxford and then once in the United States at Berkeley, and in his academic career writing about racism but never in a Jewish context. All this changed when he found himself at the Huntington, whose formality recalled his early days as an outsider at Oxford, and yet was drawn into the Nuremberg Laws story.

In my conversation with Platt, I chided him that as a leftist professor whose academic activities include editing the journal,

Social Justice, he was probably the only person who didn't know he was Jewish. Platt laughed but said that working on *Bloodlines* had caused him to reconsider his academic pursuits in light of his personal history and to think deeper about anti-Semitism as a form of racism. As a result of his book, Platt now found himself talking at synagogues and before Jewish groups and "engaging in all these interesting conversations."

Finally, in light of the Huntington's history and its handling of the Nuremberg documents, Platt has called on the library to be more open and called for it to allow a historian full access to the archives to produce a study of the institution and its history of racism, as well as other issues. Platt has since offered to "meet and do a staff workshop" to discuss the issues raised in the book. Platt's book is critical of the Huntington for never undertaking a serious investigation into the typescript's provenance—although he admits that in the absence of other claims of ownership, the Huntington's possession "prevails for the moment." The Huntington Library was originally the San Marino ranch property of Edward Huntington, whose fortunes came from his own family and by marriage and through railroads and real estate. Between 1910 and 1925, he assembled one of the great libraries of the world, acquiring the contents of more than 200 collections, including some of the world's great manuscripts, as well as books, Bibles, Shakespeare folios, presidential papers and rare first editions of poetry and fiction.

In 1919, the library was formally established. In 1925, Huntington agreed to make the library itself into a research institution, and to this day, it remains a place primarily for post-doctoral research.

In 1928, a year after Huntington's death, the estate opened itself to the public. Today, most people know the Huntington for its magnificent gardens, tearoom and Beaux-Arts art galleries, which include Gainsborough's *The Blue Boy*.

The Huntington today remains a glorious estate, and its formality and essential WASPy-ness (or goyishness, if you like) is still palpable.

No one contests the Huntington's history of exclusion as detailed by Platt—not the Skirball, not the current president of the Huntington itself, Steve Koblik, a European history and Holocaust scholar. But they see it as what the Huntington was, not what it is.

As Platt tells the story, the Huntington has evolved over the years. Robert Middlekrauf, its chief executive from 1984 to 1988, began the "democratization" of the organization, inviting more younger scholars and more women to do research there. Skotheim, president from 1988 to 2001, while still a traditionalist, recognized that the institution needed to open its doors by lending materials, inviting a wider range of scholars, as well as hosting a greater variety of exhibits and programs to attract a more diverse audience. The loan of the Nuremberg Laws to the Skirball was ostensibly done in this spirit.

Koblik joined the Huntington in 2001 and is its first Jewish president. He acknowledged in a recent phone interview that the institution's exclusionary past "was very accurate of a Pasadena-San Marino historical culture." However, he noted that San Marino itself is now sixty percent Chinese and, accordingly, very different from what it was in Huntington's day.

"Today the message [of the Huntington]," he said, "is that everybody is welcome." Koblik cited as an example a major series of African American cultural events that the Huntington has hosted over the last two years that "are SRO and eighty percent African American."

As for the Nuremberg Laws, Koblik said: "From the point of view of teaching about the Holocaust, the fact that they are at the Skirball is quite wonderful," He reaffirmed that "the purpose of the loan was to support the Skirball."

As for the question of the actual ownership of the Nuremberg Laws and how the Huntington handled them, Koblik said, "The provenance issue is not a very interesting one."

In reviewing the history of the laws, Koblik offered that "it was during wartime," the laws were "historical materials" and said Patton "liberated them." Koblik pointed out that the U.S. government seized all of the German official documents they could to preserve them. Patton, for his part, instructed the Huntington officials to put the documents in the vault, saying that he would later give instructions. "It's not unusual to get materials with restrictions." Then Patton died. "The family showed no interest in the materials."

"In this case, there was no clarity, no written agreement [regarding the laws]. They were forgotten." Koblik said that "this is not unusual," noting that only recently they had discovered a letter from Christopher Columbus in the vaults.

Koblik suggested that it was interesting to compare the situation with the laws to another case involving the Huntington concerning a photographic copy of the Dead Sea Scrolls. When Israeli researchers denied access to the scrolls to scholars, the Huntington released its photographic copy in the face of threats of suits from the Israeli government (the suits were never filed).

In the case of the laws, the Huntington's is not the sole copy (the other is in Nuremberg); its contents were widely published and are widely known. And, Koblik said, they are now on display to the public at a place where it has "more meaning."

So the laws and their provenance are "not an issue for us," he concluded.

In truth, the ownership of the Nuremberg Laws is not being contested, and no other claims of ownership have been made. As a friend said to me, "basically, it's just you stirring the pot." Fair enough. Nonetheless, I asked the opinion of E. Randol Schoenberg, the Los Angeles attorney who recently successfully recovered five paintings by Gustav Klimt from an Austrian state-owned museum on behalf of Maria Altmann.

"It would be a difficult case to decide," he said. Noting that there were cases where U.S. soldiers who looted artworks were forced to return their plunder; he acknowledged that claims could be made by the city of Eichstatt for the documents' return. The U.S. government, to which the documents should have been turned over, could also make a claim, and Schoenberg offered an opinion that the U.S. claim would be stronger than the German one. Nonetheless, he said it is possible that if the statute of limitations has run out on filing a claim, the Huntington would prevail. Schoenberg concluded that there is "no easy answer."

Still, the Huntington is not giving up the documents. Although Koblik made clear that the Huntington is not concerned about this issue, he said "our job is to collect and preserve" and reiterated that the documents are on loan and that they could consider requests from another institution, such as the Holocaust Museum in Washington. It's interesting that in my conversations with both the Skirball's Kirschner and the Huntington's Koblik, they both pointed out that for historians, the typescripts have little worth. The typescript contains no information not readily available elsewhere—and they don't in any way advance our knowledge. It was not a secret document—on the contrary, the Nuremberg Laws were immediately published all over the Germany. The Huntington's copy also is not unique—another one is in Nuremberg. The document's value resides in the signatures, both said. Its appeal is fetishistic. It is a totem.

Which is exactly why it's important to see the typescript and the signatures for oneself. The laws are just four sheets of typed paper. They look so bland that it is easy for one's eyes to glaze over just staring at them. And yes, it is their apparent banality that makes them so important.

That the Nuremberg Laws were no secret is also part of what makes them so chilling. So much discussion of the Nazi era and the final solution has to do with "secret" plans to exterminate the Jews. So often in discussing the Holocaust, one wonders: Who knew what and when? But here there are no secrets. The Jews are written off, literally in a few paragraphs.

The writing on the paper became the writing on the wall—heralding the fate of the Jews.

And then there's the fact that they are "laws." One of the main tenets of modern civilization is the regard for the moral underpinning of the rule of law. It is what we cherish about this country—and what we are willing to fight for in other countries. The just exercise of the law is, we continue to believe, the solution to global, regional and local conflicts. So it is all the more frightening to see how pseudolaws enabled the Nazi regime.

Just as the Nazis built their philosophy of National Socialism on the pseudoscience of eugenics and racial theory, they also built the legitimacy of their anti-Semitic campaign on the foundation of pseudolaws, such as the Nuremberg Laws signed not only by Hitler but by Justice Minister Gurtner.

One is reminded of the final scene in Abby Mann's *Judgment at Nuremberg,* in which Jannings, the Nazi judge, tells Haywood, the American prosecutor, that he did not imagine the Nazi's actions would lead to the death camps, and Haywood responds that "it came to that the first time you sentenced to death a man you knew to be innocent." The power of the Nuremberg Laws is that we already know what happened once they were passed.

The lesson, as I see it, is that more often than we would like to believe, things are as they seem: The Huntington, to the visitor, feels like a WASP enclave, inhospitable to outsiders—turns out it was.

The story of how the Nuremberg Laws turned up in the Huntington's vault and how Patton acquired them seemed too good to be true—turns out it was.

The Huntington's loan of the documents to the Skirball was a generous act, intended to express a new willingness on the part of the Huntington to reach out to fellow LA institutions, and to a Jewish one at that—it was.

Platt discovered that in telling a story about social justice, racism and anti-Semitism, he reconnected with his own personal history. Born Jewish, Platt discovered he was Jewish (and I don't mean that glibly—I mean that in a deeper sense).

And finally, the Nuremberg Laws were no secret—they, too, meant what they said. That Jews were no longer citizens, and their life and lives would no longer be treated as having value.

Go see the Nuremberg Laws—sooner rather than later. They are at the Skirball, but they are on loan. And the Huntington means it. They may not be there forever.

Take your children and your friends. Don't let their eyes glaze over. Let them know what they are witnessing. Tell them that laws are made by men, but governments can pervert them. Show them the power of a signed piece of paper.

May 17, 2007

ACTING THE PART

Mark Rydell

Summer movies provide thrills, chills and laughs and are more noted for their special effects and star actors than for the acting and the seriousness of their purpose. Which makes this a good time to visit with Mark Rydell, a man whose more than fifty-year career as an actor, director and producer speaks of his integrity, his commitment to being an artist and his devotion to the craft of acting.

Rydell's current offering as director is *Even Money* (now playing at a theater near you), an Altman-esque tale written by first-time screenwriter Robert Tannen about nine characters whose lives are affected by gambling.

"It's really a rare adult movie for this marketplace," Rydell told me.

Although reviews have been mixed, the cast alone, which includes Forest Whitaker, Kim Basinger, Ray Liotta, Danny DeVito, Nick Cannon and Tim Roth, is testament to Rydell's reputation for being "an actor's director."

To Rydell, who met with me recently in the West Hollywood offices of the Actor's Studio, where he is the co-artistic director (with Martin Landau), being a director is "a responsibility I take seriously"; acting is "creating behavior under imaginary circumstances," and his purpose in making a film is to "expose the truth in some way." Which is refreshing and inspiring to hear as we enter the summer blockbuster movie zone.

The Bronx-born Rydell's journey as an artist began as a jazz pianist. He studied at Julliard under Teddy Wilson and as a teenager was already playing in jazz clubs in New York and Chicago. But, as he recalled recently, "I saw a lot of my friends disintegrate as a result of drugs in the jazz world."

Afraid he might suffer the same fate, he returned to college.

One day in a Greek and Latin usage class at New York University, the teacher asked the students to etymologize the word "ornithology." Rydell began humming the Charlie Parker song of the same name and was surprised to hear the young woman seated behind him, Marilyn Katz, join in.

After they became friends, she told him he should become an actor and offered to call Sanford Meisner of the Actor's Playhouse. Rydell was admitted into the summer program, at the end of which he was offered a two-year scholarship to the acting school. (Today, Marilyn Katz is better known as half of Alan and Marilyn Bergman, one of the most successful popular lyricists and composers of our times.)

Rydell graduated the playhouse and was accepted into the Actor's Studio, the famous and prestigious acting academy where actors, directors and playwrights hone their craft over a lifetime at no expense. Over the next several years, he studied with and assisted such legendary acting teachers as Bobby Lewis, Harold Clurman, Stella Adler, Elia Kazan and Lee Strasberg. His classmates at the Actor's Studio included James Dean and Martin Landau.

To Rydell, the late forties and early fifties in New York were a modern-day Renaissance period. Jazz legends such as Charlie Parker, Art Tatum, Miles Davis and Fats Waller played in clubs along West 52nd Street. All television programming, including the live dramas, were in New York. Edward R. Murrow, Eric Sevareid and Walter Cronkite reported the news.

As for the Broadway theater, Marlon Brando was performing in Tennessee Williams' *A Streetcar Named Desire,* and Lee J. Cobb was in Arthur Miller's *Death of a Salesman.* Both performances made a lasting impression on Rydell.

Rydell's father knew Cobb and got front-row seats to *Death of a Salesman.* When the performance ended, the audience was silent, and then after fifteen to twenty seconds suddenly they erupted in thunderous applause.

Rydell went backstage, and Cobb gave Rydell two important pieces of advice: to stick with it, because "attrition is the cancer" of the acting profession; that people who are not committed enough will drop out. And he recommended that Rydell "keep training; train, train constantly because sooner or later you will get a shot and when the shot comes, you should be ready for it."

As for seeing Brando: "Brando revolutionized acting because you saw that it was possible to really experience the events [and even] the torture the part has built into it."

As Rydell says, the actors were no longer pretending to experience the events they were portraying—they experienced them.

Rydell's own acting career began in live television. A very young Sydney Lumet directed him in one episode of *Danger*. Rydell recalls that Lumet was so young, he didn't realize he was the director and asked him to get a cup of coffee; another time, to get a role on a western, he claimed to know how to ride a horse, only to find himself having to gallop past his old playhouse classmate Steve McQueen.

He earned recurring roles in the soap operas *As the World Turns* and *The Edge of Night*. His first feature role was in Reginald Rose's juvenile delinquent drama, *Crime in the Streets*, playing opposite John Cassavetes and Sal Mineo.

Nonetheless, Rydell says, "I knew early on I wanted to be a director." A director, Rydell says, is much more of a "father figure, a nurturer.": "I felt I was much more comfortable being a leader—doesn't make it better [than being an actor]. It was just more appropriate for me."

Rydell started directing *Ben Casey*, the granddaddy of medical shows, and also directed several episodes of *Gunsmoke*, as well as the first episode of *I Spy*, directing over the years, by his own estimate, fifty to sixty hours of television.

Rydell's first feature film was an adaptation of D. H. Lawrence's *The Fox*, with Sandy Dennis and Keir Dullea (as a side note: Dennis was discovered by William Gymes, a friend of my family, a Hungarian director who ran the Jan Hus theater in New York). Rydell describes it today as "the first candid sexual picture," which helped it become a runaway success. Rydell's career was launched.

At one point in our conversation Rydell confides, "I've worked with my share of major stars"—which is some understatement. Rydell's career over the last forty years includes *The Reivers* with McQueen (1967) based on the William Faulkner novel—McQueen, Rydell says, was "troubled but you couldn't take your eyes off him"; *The Cowboys* with John Wayne (1972), which Wayne told Rydell was his favorite performance; *The Rose* with Bette Midler (1979)—"one of my favorites" says Rydell; and *On Golden Pond* with Henry Fonda, Katherine Hepburn, and Jane Fonda (1981), which won an Oscar nomination for Rydell and Oscar wins for the senior Fonda, Hepburn and screenwriter Ernest Thompson. Rydell recalls that on the first day after the first scene of *On Golden Pond,* [Fonda and Hepburn] looked at me as soon as they finished." He realized that "these giants are still actors. They needed me for a mirror for the events that had occurred."

On occasion, Rydell has played roles in movies, most notably the role of Meyer Lansky in *Havana* and memorably the Jewish gangster in Robert Altman's *The Long Goodbye.*

More recently, Rydell made the HBO film, *Crime of the Century* (1996), about the Lindbergh baby kidnapping, and in 2001, *James Dean* for TNT, which launched the film career of James Franco, who won a Golden Globe for his portrayal of the troubled actor.

When Rydell was first sent Israel Horovitz's *James Dean* script, he was struck by the fact that he had known almost all the characters in it. What he most wanted to convey in the film, he says, was Dean's desperate hunger for the approval of his father.

Rydell recalls that he had met Dean in the fifties at the Actor's Studio, where they competed for roles in readings and for roles on Broadway.

"Sometimes he beat me out; sometimes I beat him out." Landau and Rydell were his friends "and he [Dean] didn't have a lot friends."

"He was incredible remarkable character—very disturbed." Rydell recalls that Dean attached himself to all of his directors who were father figures—evil ones, as well as good ones. According to Rydell, Dean hated George Stevens, who directed him in *Giant.* He loved Kazan, who directed him in *East of Eden,* but Kazan, by contrast, was impatient with Dean, and used Dean's feelings about his father to fuel the conflict in the movie.

Brando, Rydell says, suffered from the same conflict with his own father.

In truth, Rydell admits, he had his own difficulties with his father, whom he described as "a cold man" who "felt threatened" by him. Rydell left home at seventeen, joining the Army to escape his "prosaic" home. Without paging Dr. Freud, it's clear that Rydell's success at nurturing his fellow actors and leading them as a director stands in marked contrast to his experience with his own father and that through acting and the Actor's Studio he found a family.

I asked Rydell whether he felt acting had changed since the days of James Dean.

"Really good acting does not change," Rydell says. However, he says, "Craft and skills are not respected as it used to be."

In the fifties, "people studied, really studied. They worked. They went to all the teachers who were at the peak of their talent." In those days, people went to the movies to see a performance. Today, he said, "they go to see a personality."

Which is not to say that there are not talented actors. Rydell sees them in action most Fridays at the Actor's Class at the Actor's Studio. "I see great acting here of successful and unsuccessful actors." Together with Landau, Rydell feels the Actor's Studio continues to "recognize and encourage a deeper examination [in acting] than people are inclined to pursue."

Rydell says that it was his start as a musician that made him appreciate craft. "You can't pretend to be a musician, like you can pretend to be an actor—if someone says 'you're a violinist, play something'; you can't fool anybody. There are a lot of actors without training—actors who can read a script intelligently but cannot act. The difference between reading and acting is monumental."

As Rydell explains, "acting is creating behavior under imaginary circumstances; doing things—really doing things—under imaginary circumstances, and that requires a technique that you have to learn."

Rydell remains passionate about his profession. "I feel as enthusiastically as I did in my twenties," he says. He has maintained his integrity throughout his career. He has never taken on a project that "I wasn't desperate to make because of its humanity or other qualities."

The commitment to being an artist, Rydell says, is a "higher calling than being an actor or director." He has taken his role as artist and as director seriously and passionately. "What other profession," he asks, "allows you to sit people in the dark and tell them what you think is the truth for a couple of hours?"

May 31, 2007

MY FATHER WHO SAID

HE WASN'T A HERO

My father always said he wasn't a hero. "All the heroes are dead," he used to say. He said he just did what he had to under the circumstances.

My father was born in Rzeszow, Poland, as Benzion Teichholz (but he was also known as Bronislaw, Ben or Bernhard). His family later moved to Lemberg (then also known as Lvov, today as Lviv). He was the second youngest of six children; his father, Izak (Isaac), was a merchant; his mother, Henia (Helen) Glucker, came from Vienna.

My father's father was observant, a follower of the Ger rebbe. Although my father's cousin claims that my father wore payot (earlocks) as a young man, my father maintained that he practiced modern, "progressive" Judaism and wore modern dress with no beard or skullcap. He attended a Jewish gymnasium, which is akin to today's Jewish day schools, less yeshiva than a function of the quotas (numerus clausus) that limited the number of Jews allowed to attend secular and professional schools.

In Lvov, the family lived at 20 Bernstein St., the same street Sholom Aleichem had lived on. Their building was at the intersection of Bernstein and Rappoport streets, across from Lvov's oldest Jewish cemetery and down the street from the Rappoport Jewish Hospital.

Early on, my father established himself in business. From 1936 to 1939 he was a director of Polski-Lloyd A.G., the Polish arm of Lloyd's of London, involved in the import-export business. His father was a merchant, and his eldest brother, Josef, worked in a family business they ran from the home (I found their telephone number listed in the 1936 Lvov phone book). Another brother, Aron, was a banker. A sister, Adella (or Bella), married and moved to Tarnopol, where she ran the Orbis Travel agency.

In 1939, as a consequence of the Molotov-Ribbentrop pact between the Soviet Union and Nazi Germany, Poland was divided, with the Nazis invading and conquering the western half, while eastern Poland, including Lvov, came under Soviet rule.

Thousands of Jews fled German-occupied Poland, many arriving in Lvov as refugees. My father, along with a friend, immediately became involved in the Jewish community's relief efforts, providing clothing, food, housing and financial assistance for homeless families.

The Soviets made him a nochelnik, a foreman, in charge of a lumber operation.

His experiences with the Soviets would make him a lifelong anti-communist.

In 1941, the Nazis conquered the rest of Poland and, with the help of local Polish police and Polish and Ukrainian collaborators, soon established a ghetto in Lvov and ordered the Jews to establish their own leadership organization, the Judenrat. My father was appointed to a committee of the Judenrat that dealt with accommodating Jews who'd been dislocated from their homes. He would later say that he was eventually asked to head the Judenrat, but as the first leader had been shot and the second hung himself, he declined the position and escaped from Lvov.

In another account, my father related that on September 19, 1941, he left Lvov as part of a labor detail assigned by the Nazis to cut down lumber in the forest.

My father was able to bribe a guard and flee.

As a reprisal for his escape, the Nazis rounded up his parents, brothers and sisters and sent them to their death either at the local Janovska concentration camp (most likely) or from there to the Belzec extermination camp.

My father joined the underground, fighting in a partisan group called Skole-Lawdezne. They attempted to procure arms, which were costly and often turned out to be old and/or defective. On occasion, the non-Jews who sold them those arms and supplies or who even fought alongside them in the resistance nevertheless denounced them to the authorities. They were in constant danger.

My father used to tell a story that around Christmas 1941, he was up in the mountains starving, and the group approached a Polish farmer, asking him to sell them some food. The farmer refused, and they later took one of his cows. The farmer denounced them to the police and the Nazis.

The slaughtered cow left a trail of blood, which the Nazis and police followed. There was a battle in which many of the members of the partisan unit were killed or captured. My father escaped across the border at Munkacz into Hungary, where the border police promptly arrested him.

Hungary was not yet under Nazi rule, but the border police were vigorously on the lookout for illegal refugees and members of partisan units. For three days, my father was beaten and tortured by the Hungarian police. He was beaten so badly that he had to be taken to a hospital in Budapest to recover.

At the hospital, he was visited by members of the Jewish community involved in rescue work. They arranged with a guard there to have him taken outside to get cigarettes, and once in the streets of Budapest, my father managed to escape.

In early 1942 in Budapest, he joined the Polish Rescue Committee, heading the Polish-Jewish Refugee Committee with Siegfried Moses. In April, 1943, he reported to the Hungarian leadership about the fate of Poland's Jews and the specific steps of the Nazi's plans for Jewish extermination.

The response was that what occurred in Poland could not happen in Hungary.

Nonetheless, his account was forwarded to Gerhard Riegner and Jewish leaders in Switzerland and to the Jewish leadership in Istanbul.

After the Nazis arrived in Budapest in April 1944, he operated under the code name "Glick," leading a technical unit of 120 Jewish men and women (many of them teenagers). They built bunkers, served as couriers and smuggled people and arms across the Hungarian border. They also forged identity papers and distributed false documents. My father's work brought him into close contact with such Hungarian Jewish leaders as Rudolf Kastner, Joel Brand and his wife, Hansi Brand, as well as Moshe Kraus and Otto Komoly.

On two occasions, he was arrested but managed to escape from both the Tollonhaz and Marko Street prisons. When members of the underground were arrested and tortured and asked to reveal their leader, they answered "Glick" (regardless of whether he worked with them or not). As a result, the Nazis and Hungarian Arrow Cross police put a price of 500 marks on my father's head for his capture, arrest or death.

For many months, my father never slept twice in the same apartment and was constantly on the move. At one point, they had to move him to the surrounding countryside because the search for him became too intense and too dangerous to other members of the unit.

Forging identity documents also caused him to meet with Raoul Wallenberg. When Wallenberg issued 100 Swedish protective passes, my father's group would forge several hundred copies. Concerned that the Nazis would see a problem in there being so many "Swedish" citizens of Hungary, Wallenberg requested a meeting with my father. My father explained that the more Swedish passes, real or forged, the more lives saved. Wallenberg assented to the forgery operation.

In later years, my father would say that he admired Wallenberg for putting his own life at risk when he didn't have to. He witnessed Wallenberg standing up to the Nazi authorities and personally going to the train transport platform to pull people off the trains and out of the lines that meant certain death, declaring them "Swedish citizens."

The last time he saw Wallenberg was in January 1945, a few days after the Russian army liberated Budapest. A few days later, he heard that the Russians had arrested Wallenberg. My father always believed that Wallenberg died in a Russian jail, not only because his experience with the Russians had taught him of their brutality but also because he knew of their ineptitude and believed that were Wallenberg alive, he would have somehow sent a message from his cell to the right channels to free him.

After the war, my father went to Vienna, where he convinced the occupying authorities to designate the former Rothschild Hospital, which had been used as a prison during the war, as a center for Jewish refugees under his leadership.

The International Committee for Jewish refugees and Former Inmates of Concentration Camps was created as a result, with my father as its president, to represent the Jews in Austria.

Between 1945 and 1951, the Rothschild Hospital would help more than 200,000 Jews get medical attention and vocational training and aid them in finding new lives by providing emigration visas. Men, women, families, orphaned children, famous rabbis, the religious and the atheists, the young and the old, the infirm and the healthy—all passed through the Rothschild Hospital.

As president, he wielded great power. He dealt with the four occupying powers --and the American Army officials in particular—as well as Jewish and American relief agencies, such as the Joint Distribution Committee and the Red Cross. He also was involved with securing visas to foreign countries.

I am under the impression that my father earned little salary for doing all this, but at a time when many survivors had nothing, he had an apartment, a car and access to supplies and rations. He was a big shot—"the king of the Jews."

As president of the International Committee, he attended the first post-war Zionist Congress in Basel, Switzerland, in 1946. During this period, he was also active in the Briha, facilitating illegal immigration to Palestine, helping to arrange transports and smuggle arms, for which Israel awarded him the

Ot Haganah in 1967 and the State Fighter's Award in 1988. In 1949, he was one of the pallbearers when Theodore Herzl was disinterred in Vienna and flown to be buried in the new State of Israel. In 1952, he emigrated to the United States.

All this happened before I was born. In my memory, however, the father I was born to was an immigrant, a greenhorn, a Polish Jew who wanted to have nothing to do with his Polish heritage (asked where he came from, he would often say "Galicia" or some term that referred to the Austro-Hungarian empire, or he might say "Lemberg," as if the city were a country). My mother, a Hungarian, had met my father in Vienna after the war. They were trying to make a life in New York, trying to make a living in America, the best country in the world.

What did I know of my father's experience during the Shoah? How did I learn it? What did my father tell me and when? How did it affect me then and to this day?

For the first five years of my life, we lived in an apartment on the Upper West Side of Manhattan on West End Avenue. All the other kids I knew and played with were the children of European Jews. We lived there because another Polish Jewish couple had told my parents about the apartment. Most of my parents' friends were either Hungarian, Polish or Austrian survivors. My maternal grandmother, Adrienne Bogner, lived two blocks away.

Even at that early age, I had some notion, some vague consciousness, that a war had occurred in Europe. The Nazis were the bad guys. We, the former Europeans, the Jewish ones, had outsmarted them, had bested the German Nazis and won (I was a little confused about Germans and Nazis, because all the parents I knew spoke German but were not Nazis, but all the Nazis spoke German).

I knew that my father had played some role in this, that he had been a spy for the good guys. I had some impression that he had blown up bridges or committed acts of sabotage against the Nazis. I can say that even as a 5-year-old, my understanding of what had occurred was not that 6 million Jews had died, but that 6 million survived and that the Nazis had been defeated.

My father conveyed a sense that, having survived as he had, having accomplished what he had, there was no challenge he could not meet. And no goal that, as a native-born American citizen, I could not achieve. I sensed that my father was an important person. Along West End Avenue, I recall people stopping my father and greeting him with respect as "Herr president." On occasion at the Eclair pastry shop on West 72nd Street, the cashiers would not accept payment from him—he would insist—or they would make him a gift of some extra pastries. A woman told me, "Your father saved my life."

But my father did not talk about his life, his experiences. His parents and brothers and sisters were "lost" in the war (no one called it the Holocaust yet).

Later, when I was in high school, he started to speak to students in public high schools and in colleges and would take me along. There, sitting in a classroom, was how I first heard about his wartime experiences (I also often typed up or helped him write those speeches—those were some of my first writing assignments).

My father tended to talk about the war in generalizations ("In 1939 Germany invaded Poland") and with sweeping conclusions ("there was resistance—in every place; in small places, small resistance; in large places, large resistance").

His message was that the Jews did fight back against all odds, under impossible circumstances.

He would tell of the ghettoization of Lvov, of how people were sent to the "East" never to return, their families duped by postcards saying all was well—which they later learned had been signed moments before the families were murdered. He told of how he escaped from Budapest and fought with the partisans; how at every step they were betrayed. How no one wanted to believe what was to occur; how no one wanted to help, and yet how they fought back as best they could. And he would always say, "There are no heroes; the heroes are all dead."

He offered little in the way of personal details to his audiences or to me for that matter, just the historical facts as he experienced them. He did not talk about his family members—never mentioned the names of his brothers and sisters, never described them. Those details were taboo.

Every father is a hero to his child. Every parent is also an oppressor to his child. In my case, the two were complicated by my father's heroic status and the notion that his suffering demanded that we ignore or excuse his anger. Imagine thinking that your father, the Holocaust hero, was behaving like a Nazi—that was the worst, most transgressive thought that ever flashed through my young mind.

My father, having been right about so much, having survived by his certainty in every situation, remained certain about everything. Worldly as he was, he had a narrow, very pragmatic prism through which he viewed every situation, and our normal parent-child differences were repressed, at least on my part, by my need to please him.

My father had nightmares—while sleeping, he often talked in foreign languages, and, on occasion, he shouted or let out a wail. This was just a fact of my childhood, something frightening and strangely haunting—never really explained, just sort of dismissed.

I understood that this was the residue of my father's experience, and it was not to be discussed. Similarly, although my father had a dry sense of humor and was generally upbeat, in private he sometimes erupted into rages, hurling insults.

Other times when he was angry, he would just turn off and go silent. This, too, was written off—excused or explained by the past he didn't discuss.

To some extent, I felt that having lost his parents so young, so traumatically, he did not really know how to be a parent—he was not the sort to play ball with me or do many of the typical father-son activities. This was my theory for many years, but it was not really based on the facts—one day I realized that my father had already reached his thirties when he last saw his parents.

Still, at a remove of several decades and as a parent myself, I wonder about my father's anger and about his guilt. And about the guilt the rest of us shared over what he had endured.

My father was close with his family, but clearly he was rebellious. Even before the war, he rebelled to play soccer on Saturdays, and eventually he rebelled against the strictures of their faith. He was not the son who worked in the business with his father. He went off to do something else. And when the time came, he was the one who fled the ghetto. Did they approve? Were they supportive? I was never sure.

The Nazis murdered his parents and brothers and sisters— using his escape as their excuse—most likely they would have been murdered a few weeks later with the rest of the Jews in the Lvov ghetto. Nonetheless, did my father feel guilty? Did he feel in some way responsible? Or was he just angry and repressing the anger over their deaths? I can't tell you.

I can remember that we always had to tread lightly on those days when he lit the Yizkor memorial candles for his family. He was in a funk on those days. Those candles glowing in the dark spooked me.

I also know that he sought to protect me. He felt the adult working world could wait—he was against my having summer jobs or doing part-time work when I was in school—I should study, play or do sports instead. Although he was a business-man, he didn't really want me to learn about business from him. He wanted me to be a leader, an elected official perhaps, certainly a lawyer. He didn't want me to work for others—bet-ter to have my own office and not be beholden to others. For my father, being a real estate broker, builder and manager was work—that was his business. His spare time was spent working for the Democratic Club, helping his local synagogue, working for Jewish charities—that was what he loved. He continued to work with the Joint Distribution Committee and ORT, as well as the Anti-Defamation League.

Although my father could be warm, loving, even tender, he was also stiff and formal, somewhat cut off. There was not a lot of discussion of feelings. In fact, as an adult, my father would often call to have lunch, saying he had something important to discuss. I would go feeling anxious, with some concern about some revelation—only for us to place our order and sit silently through it.

I would ask: "Was there something you needed to tell me?" He would answer that he just wanted to see me, see how I was doing.

Just as archaeological digs must first excavate the more re-cent civilizations before getting to the older ones—interest in my father's history seemed to proceed in reverse chronological order. At first, journalists and historians were interested in his work in the Briha, and many of the Holocaust survivors knew him because of his position in Vienna and his work at the Rothschild Hospital. Later, when Wallenberg became a known figure, interest surged in my father's underground work in Budapest.

As early as 1947, he was approached about writing his memoirs, but he couldn't quite do it. Over the years, he was interviewed by prominent journalists, including I.F. Stone, Meyer Levin, Ruth Gruber and Elenore Lester, and historians such as Yehuda Bauer and Randolph Braham.

He tried to dictate his own memoirs, and at a much later date I tried to help him organize and write them. He gave oral and video testimony for archives. However, he could never really describe the details of what he experienced—they didn't seem important to him, he couldn't recall them. His talent was to organize—to deal with the problems facing him, to lead the people surrounding him, to help others, to do what needed to be done.

Nonetheless, he appears in the accounts of almost a dozen works of history, including Braham's *The Politics of Genocide,* (1981); Bauer's *Flight and Rescue* (1967); and Thurston Clarke and Frederick E. Werbell's *Lost Hero: The Mystery of Raoul Wallenberg* (1982). In 1985, NBC broadcast a miniseries, *Wallenberg: A Hero's Story,* written by Gerald Green ("The Last Angry Man"), starring Richard Chamberlain as Wallenberg and featuring Ralph Arliss as Teicholz, one of the Jewish resistance leaders.

My father died in 1993. In 1995, I traveled to Lvov, now part of Ukraine. While there, I was able to see the street he lived on, the apartment building he lived in, the Jewish community hall where he attended meetings, the headquarters of the Judenrat, and the entrance to the ghetto.

I visited the Janovska camp and saw the field where his family was most likely murdered and said Kaddish there; I also saw the train transport from which others he knew were sent to their death at the Belzec extermination camp.

At the entrance to the former ghetto, there is now a Holocaust memorial. I arranged to have a memorial plaque placed there in the names of his parents and siblings.

While in Lvov, I also visited the municipal archives, where I found a 1936 business directory listing Izak Teichholz as kupciek (merchant) and Josef Teichholz as working at the same address (there was also a listing for Wolf Teichholz working there, who I would later learn was a cousin).

I also found the 1939 municipal voting records. To my amazement, there, in clear type, in ordered columns, were my grandparents, uncles and aunts—and my father.

There were surprises in that list. I learned, for example, that though we had always celebrated my father's birthday on Feb. 20—turns out it was in July (so much for thinking he was a Pisces!). His passport said he was born in 1914; turns out it was 1908 (he always said that the passport was a few years wrong, but he never said how much). Imagine being so unsentimental about your birth date as to celebrate it on a completely different day and never tell your wife and children the actual date.

Moreover, the list included only four Teichholz children, including my father.

My best guess, and it is only that, is that his sister, Adella (or Bella), was already married and living in Tarnopol, so she didn't appear. As for the missing sibling—my father mentioned a sister who was married and died in London during the war—I had asked my father several times how he knew she had died, but he just dismissed my questions.

Finally, the document said they all arrived in Lvov in 1930, which would mean that, in fact, my father didn't grow up in Lemberg, as he said, but arrived there as an adult. So that, too, is a mystery.

In recent years, I've also recovered transcripts of interviews my father gave to the American Jewish Congress as part of its oral history project, as well as to Bauer and Braham. In each, I found details not found elsewhere, small slivers of his story he had not shared elsewhere in a cohesive way.

Today, I know more about my father's history than I did when he was alive. Sometimes, I wish I could interview him now, but I fear that although my questions might be more informed, I still would not get better answers from him.

A few years ago, I had a rather surreal experience. While doing some research on the Web, I discovered Hebrew University in Jerusalem had in its archive an interview with my father—Bauer had donated his papers, including his interview with my father for his book on the Briha. I e-mailed them asking them for a transcript, and they sent me one.

Almost every third word was marked "unintelligible." I e-mailed them again, to ask for an audiotape of the interview and to offer to correct and complete their transcript. Several weeks later, a manila envelope containing a cassette appeared in my mailbox.

I then had the strange experience of hearing my father's voice again, some twelve years after his death, and the even stranger experience of finding myself frustrated by his maddeningly opaque manner of talking and irritated with his Polish circumlocutions, pauses and nonanswer answers. I understood every word he said, and in the end, the transcript was no wiser for it.

My father's heroism, his altruism was not, I believe, a matter of any conscious philosophy. It was part of who he was, part of his DNA. He was active in relief work before the Nazis entered Lvov, and he continued to be involved in charity work throughout his life in the United States.

As for his Jewish identity, he didn't keep kosher, he wasn't Sabbath observant, but as I have often remarked, he never breathed a breath that wasn't Jewish. He supported Israel before it was a state, traveled there often and was totally committed to its existence and its support, but he chose not to live there.

Am I the product of nurture or nature?

My father's experience in Poland and Hungary, his work in the underground and later in Vienna at the Rothschild Hospital and in the Briha confirmed his self-confidence and his belief in his own abilities as, he put in one oral history, as having "a genius for organizing." He had tremendous self-confidence and certainty. At the same time, he had the quality, shared by many successful businessmen, of having little attachment to the facts beyond the opportunities they present in the moment—and a great ability to move on to the next question.

By contrast, what my father did not give out—I seek out. I want to know the details. I see the complexity of every situation, the good and the bad. I empathize with each story. I find myself attached to facts and to the past.

Eager to search them out, nail them down—yet they remain awash in the gray zones. Yet I have a sentimental side and a desire to please and be liked that would be alien to my father. He would just do. I don't like confrontations and prefer to organize my thoughts on paper.

In my writing, I am the translator of experience, the witness, the reporter of stories, seeking to place them in context and search out meaning. This is part of my reaction to my father's experience. But is this so different from so many other Jewish writers born after the Holocaust?

Do I support Israel or do charitable work only because of my father? No. Is doing so part of my DNA, part of my personality? Yes. Is doing so part of my patrimony? Yes.

In my professional life, I have consistently written about Jewish subjects regardless of the publication or the ostensible subject of the book or article (literature, fashion or retailing for example), and I have consistently found a home writing for Jewish publications.

But my father did not encourage me to write about "Jewish" subjects. To the contrary, this is a world I created for myself, out of my own interests. I won't say that my father was not supportive of my being a journalist or writer. He just didn't think being a writer was a good business. He wanted me to go to law school, and I did. But I also went to journalism school.

What I know for sure is that my father gave me a sense of Jewish history—a direct connection to the history and fate of the Jewish people that feels very personal to me. At the Passover seder, saying that I was in Egypt is something I feel deep in my soul. The Purim story is part of a chain of events that I recognize, a chain linked to my father's experience, and that continues to this day. And, yes, I feel a sense of obligation, as well.

At a certain point, one becomes an adult, or at least an individual separated from one's parents, able to see them as human, imperfect, with faults. It doesn't lessen the respect, just creates different boundaries.

It is difficult to grow up the son of a famous father, just as it is sometimes difficult for plants to grow in the shadow of another plant that receives so much sunlight. One struggles to forge a separate identity—yet.

Yet. Here I am, a grown man, married, in middle age, father of a daughter, still writing about my father.

In the last year, I was asked to write about him for a Wallenberg Web site and to contribute a page about him for the 100th anniversary of the New York synagogue to which he belonged. I also updated and expanded his entry in the new edition of the Encyclopaedia Judaica. And I have written this essay.

I am a writer. I witness. I put my words on paper to inform but also to prove that I exist. I am all this, in spite of—but certainly because of, my father.

My father was Bruce Teicholz who, given that he is dead, I can say was a hero.

June 14, 2007

THE SALONISTAS OF LA

Great ideas and great literature are being championed, promoted and supported in Los Angeles, in public and private forums, in private homes and public spaces, through the age-old medium of conversation.

Several years ago, the Jewish Museum in New York mounted an exhibition called *The Power of Conversation: Jewish Women and Their Salons.* Focusing on women such as Henriette Herz in 1780s Berlin, Genevieve Straus in 1890s Paris and Salka Viertel in 1930s Santa Monica, the exhibition demonstrated the critical role these women played in the culture of their times and in promoting the work of such writers as Oscar Wilde, Marcel Proust, Bertolt Brecht and Thomas Mann.

Today in Los Angeles, the three Jewish women profiled below—Andrea Grossman, Louise Steinman, and Julie Robinson—have created their own twenty-first century versions of the salon. Whereas once the salon was a private, exclusive gathering, today it has become far more democratic.

Grossman runs Writer's Bloc, a nonprofit organization that, as its Web site declares, "is dedicated to producing provocative, fun and entertaining programs that feature the most interesting writers and thinkers in our cultural landscape." Louise Steinman is the director of the ALOUD Series at the Los Angeles Public Library's Central Library, which declares itself, on its Web site, as "the place to exchange ideas with fellow citizens and to learn from outstanding thinkers and artists across a wide variety of disciplines." And, finally, Julie Robinson is a book group leader whose company, Literary Affairs, promises to take readers "beyond the book" and who in addition to hosting book groups in private homes, now also leads book groups at the Beverly Hills Tennis Club, Wilshire Boulevard Temple and Sinai Temple, and organizes author events and even literary travel experiences.

Today, almost every cultural institution hosts a reading series. What the salonistas described below have discovered is no longer a secret: Los Angeles, in spite of—or perhaps because of—its reputation as the world capital of scripted entertainment and the purveyor of "reality" entertainment, is filled with passionate readers who hunger for literary fiction, ideas and conversation.

Writer's Bloc: Great Writers in Public Forums

Since 1996, Writer's Bloc has offered up a heady mix of writers and interviewers in conversation. I can't remember when I attended my first Writer's Bloc event, but soon those familiar black-and-white postcards started piling up in my mailbox, announcing one more amazing event after another.

Over the years, the writers who've appeared include a Who's Who of contemporary culture, including Alice Walker, John Irving, Scott Turow, Isabel Allende, Gore Vidal, Nora Ephron, Richard Ford, Mona Simpson, Steve Martin, Michael Ondatje, Norman Mailer, Joan Didion and pretty much anyone you can imagine being interested in hearing.

Some unforgettable evenings I've attended include seeing El-more Leonard and Martin Amis (together!) or, more recently, Bob Woodward being interviewed by John Dean.

Although the venues for the events change (they've been held at such different locales as the WGA theater, The Fine Arts Theatre, the auditorium at the Wiesenthal Center and Temple Emmanuel in Beverly Hills), they are consistent in providing a sense of drama and excitement—they are always events.

I've been to some that were sold-out/standing-room only, and others where a few dozen fans spread themselves throughout the rows. But without doubt, the most enthusiastic fan at each is always Andrea Grossman, who is the founder and one-woman band behind Writer's Bloc.

Grossman grew up in Beverly Hills, and is a graduate of Beverly Hills High, of UCLA as an English major and of USC's Annenberg School, where she received a graduate degree in communications management. She worked in corporate marketing, in pay-TV programming for the legendary Z Channel, as well as for Select TV, and worked in Democratic Party Fundraising.

Grossman discovered her calling when she suggested to the Friends of English UCLA support group that they bring in authors of cultural interest. After Isabel Allende's appearance, Grossman realized two things: First, "that certain authors should be speaking not just in bookstores, but in a public forum," and second, what Grossman calls "'The *Sesame Street*' effect"—where if you get one great person to appear, then it becomes OK, or even mandatory, for others to do so.

Grossman saw "a real need for mainstream great writers to talk about their ideas in a friendly forum" that was "not stuffy, not academic, just fun." Out of that conviction, Writer's Bloc was born.

From the start, Grossman's intention was to set the standard extremely high, to get great writers involved. For her first real Writer's Bloc event, Joan Didion was interviewed by Robin Abcarian of the Los Angeles Times. That certainly set the bar.

Over the years, Elmore Leonard has appeared four times; Norman Mailer, three times; Gore Vidal three times; and Steve Martin, Calvin Trillin, and Harry Shearer have also made several appearances.

Writer's Bloc is a nonprofit. Grossman explained that while on occasion authors have received fees for appearing, most of the time they do not. Tickets are twenty dollars, and authors usually stay after to sign books, which are sold on the premises.

Although Grossman told me that her "real love is fiction," her programs frequently feature nonfiction writers. She admits to "being real interested in political figures."

Grossman confessed that although "sometimes [running] Writer's Bloc can be frustrating, with problems and issues to handle," she loves the programming part of it. What she loves most is an event where "there's great drama and great theater."

She acknowledges that in Los Angeles the challenge is to get people out of their homes. That, too, is Grossman's standard: "I only do a program if I would get in my car and fight traffic [to go see it].

As for high points from the last nine seasons, Grossman cites an evening with John Le Carre reading from "Smiley" and telling stories as unforgettable; a Garrison Keillor program, right after September 11, where she recalls that "people were desperate for community" and Keillor got everyone singing. "It was fantastic," she says.

Then there was the night when George Carlin "became emotional and quite distraught remembering certain aspects of his childhood and his comic heroes."

Grossman concludes: "To have such figures who have had such a significant impact on our culture—to see them so intimately is invaluable."

For more information on Writer's Bloc, visit http://www.writersblocpresents.com.

LOUISE STEINMAN AND THE
HEARTH OF LOS ANGELES

Louise Steinman's route to leading the Los Angeles Public Library's Central Library's cultural programs has been one of much "serendipity." She grew up in Los Angeles, attended Reed College in Portland, where she received her bachelor's in literature, and received a master's in interdisciplinary arts from San Francisco State University.

"Interdiscplinary" would be a good description for her artistic and writing career.

Steinman has created performances and dance theater works for her SO & SO & SO & SO company (co-founded with Susan Banyas); she has written works of criticism such as *The Knowing Body: The Artist as Contemporary Performance;* and she wrote an autobiographical memoir *The Souvenir: A Daughter Discovers Her Father's War.* On her Web site, Steinman states that her work "frequently addresses issues of memory, history and reconciliation."

In 1986, the Los Angeles Public Library's downtown central branch was victim to two incidents of arson, which closed the library. Shortly after its reopening in 1993, Steinman, who had been cultural director of Barnsdall Park, was asked to direct public programs for the library.

She was hired by Gary Ross, the Hollywood director of such films as "Dave" and "Seabiscuit," who was president of the Library Board of Commissioners. He had grand ideas for the library's programs (Steinman recalls Ross saying "Let's get Gorbachev!").

In the beginning, Steinman admits "the learning curve was very steep." They had few resources, limited support for ads, marketing, and outreach, and the audiences at times were limited to handful of people.

Yet things began to change. "Downtown started to happen," Steinman said. The library foundation hired an outreach manager, publicist Regina Mangum. Steinman brought her curiosity, her interdisciplinary interests, and her sense of performance not only to programming what is now "Aloud" but also to the library itself, and the space where the events are held, the Mark Taper Auditorium.

Steinman was particularly captivated by observing how people interacted with the space. "The library is a welcome space," Steinman said recently. "People think of this space as the hearth of the city."

Aloud hosts between seventy and eighty-five events a year, by Steinman's estimation. All are free (on occasion Aloud has charged a five dollar fee for a performing arts program, but they have not done so in a while). Reservations are not required but are suggested, as events sometimes sell out.

Steinman was quick to point out that in fact she does not work for the city, or for the library, but for the Library Foundation of Los Angeles, which is a nonprofit organization founded to help secure private support for the library.

Accordingly, the events are provided at no cost to the library or the city (and accordingly at no tax cost to us). (I will disclose here that I recently interviewed novelist Nathan Englander for the *Aloud* series and received an honorarium for doing so.) The Library Foundation, for its part, does raise funds, and the public is encouraged to become library foundation members and/or make donations to the foundation.

When asked to list some highlights, Steinman responded, "there have been so many deeply moving [programs]." While first recalling those memorable speakers who were no longer among us, such as W.G. Sebald, Susan Sontag, and August Wilson, Steinman also recalled stirring debates and discussions, such as Sam Harris and Reza Aslan on "Can Faith and Reason Co-exist?" (moderated by Jonathan Kirsch); an evening devoted to the Polish poet Adam Zagajewski; David Milch (of "Deadwood" fame) and William Deveareaux, a scholar of the West, in a free-wheeling conversation that Steinman describes as "brilliant"; Buddhist scholar Robert Thurman with director David O. Russell, who had been his student at Amherst.

An eclectic list to be sure, but Steinman's credo is that "all subjects are contained in the library and all subjects are fair game [for ALOUD]."

For more information, visit: www.lfla.org/aloud/.

LITERARY AFFAIRS

The Salon in Your Living Room

"My whole concept is to take readers beyond the book," Julie Robinson, book group leader par excellence, told me recently. "To create an experience based on great literature."

Robinson is a great example of how doing what you love and following your passion can not only become a life, but a living as well.

Robinson grew up in New York and Massachusetts and came to Los Angeles after graduating college. As a stay-at-home mom, she was always reading. She would often arrive at her children's pre-school book-in-hand; the other moms would ask her for book recommendations.

She went back to UCLA to take English literature courses and formed a book group that met in her living room. With the help of Doug Dutton of Dutton's Bookstore in Brentwood and writer Diane Leslie, who often hosted writer events at Dutton's, Robinson began to host book clubs. What began as a hobby, according to Robinson, soon evolved into her business, "Literary

Affairs." When she began, people said to her: "Just having coffee klatches—that's not a business."

Today Robinson personally runs twenty-three book groups a month. She has two people who work for her, and she is training facilitators to lead other groups, such as a kids' group for children, beginning in fourth grade, and a mother/daughter reading group.

Her groups usually have eight to sixteen members, however, since Robinson charges by the group, not the person, there are clients who pay for her to have lunch with them and a friend and talk about a novel (that goes for around $250).

In the decade since Robinson launched Literary Affairs, book groups have not only proliferated, but are recognized now as an important way for publishers and authors to market their work. Robinson is now regularly courted by publishers.

The reason is simple: book groups are overwhelmingly female. "Women are the highest percentage of book buyers," Robinson told me. "Even many of the books that men and children read are purchased for them by women."

This is all the more true for literary fiction.

Robinson continues to believe that "the market is out there for fiction." Her attitude is that "Every book is of value for a different reason." Some for the quality of their prose; others for being a window into a different world, and others still for the lessons they impart; Robinson cited, Elif Shafak's *The Bastard of Istanbul* as a book where her readers "learning about the Armenian Genocide" is more than "enough to get from a book."

My friend Teri Hertz, who first told me about Robinson, has been part of a book group for several years that recently turned to Robinson as facilitator. Hertz has been impressed by how creative Robinson is at creating an informed discussion and bringing a book and its subject to life.

Robinson has expanded into doing series at country clubs, where she invites professors to provide context to their readings—she recently hosted a luncheon series on the books of Jane Austen, and this summer several of her groups are going to tackle Tolstoy's epic *War and Peace* over the course of three months.

She leads book groups at Wilshire Boulevard Temple and Sinai Temple. She recently hosted an event where she interviewed Swedish-born author Linda Olsson, author of *Astrid and Veronika* at Lief, a Swedish antique store where Swedish cocktails and appetizers were served. Similarly, she hosted an event at the Italian Cultural Institute for Elizabeth Gilbert's *Eat, Pray, Love.* Robinson is constantly evolving the way she can extend the literary experience for her clients and has begun offering literary travel tours as well.

Nevertheless, what Robinson is proudest of is that she created her business as a single mom and has never had to sacrifice her role as a mother. For example, she never set her book group gatherings before 7:30 p.m., so she could be at home for dinner. As her family needs have evolved, she has grown her business.

Robinson believes that, if after attending a book club session she has facilitated "you walk away thinking more…and if you are more conscious, then I did my job."

June 14, 2007

DINING GOLD

"The plov is great."

Jonathan Gold, the *LA Weekly*'s restaurant critic and the 2007 winner of the Pulitzer Prize for Criticism, e-mailed me the above about Uzbekistan (the restaurant on La Brea, not the country), where we were planning to meet.

He assumed, of course, that I knew what plov is—I didn't then, but I do now; it's a rice dish, like pilaf, usually made with lamb and cooked in a pot. It's common in Turkmenistan, Uzbekistan and Kazakhstan, but not in Los Angeles. Gold has described it as "the grandfather of all pilafs, dense and slightly oily, more like dried rice than ordinary pilaf, spiked with long-cooked carrots and crisp-edged chunks of lamb, flavored with a peculiar brand of Uzbek cumin seed that is halfway between cumin and caraway."

The Pulitzer judges noted Gold's knowledge of and enthusiasm for dishes that might seem obscure, praising his "zestful, wide-ranging restaurant reviews, which express the delight of an erudite eater." He is the first food critic to be awarded a Pulitzer, and his was the first won by the *LA Weekly*, an alternative newspaper edited by Laurie Ochoa, who is also Gold's wife. That must have been a good week in their home.

Gold has been writing about food for more than two decades—his column, *Counter Intelligence,* began appearing in the *LA Weekly* in 1986, moved to the *Los Angeles Times* in the early 1990s and then returned to the *Weekly*. (When I first moved to LA more than a decade ago, I was given two essential items: a Thomas guide and a copy of his book, *Counter Intelligence*.) He has single-handedly expanded where and what Los Angelenos will eat—educating our palates about food high and low, dear and cheap, comforting and downright scary.

Jonathan Gold's writing brims with wit and flair and is fun to read, whether you ever eat a dish he describes or not. He is the Walt Whitman of LA food: His reviews contain the multitudes of our cuisines; he is our West Coast Calvin Trillin, intrepid in his exploration and reportage; an S. J. Perelman of food writing, threading his work with pop culture references that crackle with gusto.

Gold describes himself as "an LA guy through and through."

As we ripped into some Uzbek bread, which resembled a bialy the size of a plate, Gold recounted that until his family moved to the Westside when he was 10, he lived south of Baldwin Hills.

"My dad loved to eat," Gold recalled, saying that his parents "went to every restaurant," including such long-forgotten haunts as Edna Earle's Fog Cutter Restaurant on La Brea and Perino's on Wilshire. Their shul was Wilshire Boulevard Temple, and in keeping with reform tradition, Sunday nights were reserved for Chinese food. "Our local was Café de Chine on Fairfax" and, after that closed, Twin Dragon on Pico. "When I was in sixth grade, I won all kinds of contests for writing poems about food." Given that Gold's work was once posted on the bulletin board at Culver Elementary, you could say the writing was already on the wall, but early on it was music, not food, that drove Gold.

Gold studied composition and conducting at UCLA. He played the cello. However, when, as he puts it, "adolescence hit late and it hit hard," Gold became obsessed with punk rock. He began spending his time in bands, going to clubs—for a while he even ran the Anti-Club in Hollywood (which the *LA Weekly* listed in its twentieth anniversary issue as one of their readers' top twenty LA clubs of the last decades).

One benefit of the musician's schedule (sound check at 6:00 p.m., on stage at 11:00) was that there was always loads of time to kill, and Gold spent it going to restaurants.

In his senior year in high school, he had a girlfriend whose mother was a physics professor and, in his estimation, "a fantastic, fantastic, Chinese cook." He arranged to have dinner at their house as often as possible. He began exploring new places in Chinatown and Monterey Park. "It was just incredible, the freshness of the food," he recalls. "You could go to the same place thirty times in a row and never get the same dish."

He became obsessive in his eating habits. "As a lark, when I was twenty, I decided to eat at every restaurant on Pico Boulevard." Nonetheless, he says he still "never thought of myself as a food person."

Gold supported himself by proofreading, working first at a law firm in Century City and then at the *LA Weekly*, but he still thought of himself as a music person. When he first wrote for the *Weekly* it was about opera and classical music.

One day, however, Jay Levin, then the Weekly's editor, asked Gold if he wanted to edit the biannual restaurant issue. "I turned out to be good at it," Gold said.

Nonetheless, Gold continued to write about music—for Rolling Stone, Spin, Vanity Fair and Details (where he was a contributing editor). During the 1990s, he got to spend time with Nirvana but was often the go-to-guy for pieces on West Coast rap, writing about NWA , Eazy E, Dr. Dre, Ice Cube, and Young MC.

At one point, Gold spent so much time around Snoop Dog that he "felt like Boswell to his Dr. Johnson." Would that have made him the Dizzle to Fo Shizzle?

Gold also wrote about heavy metal for the *LA Times*. However, late one night in the 1990s, when the lead singer of a band told Gold that he'd passed on going to Columbia to move to New York's Chinatown to pursue his rock-and-roll dreams, Gold's reaction was, "Your poor parents!" He knew then it was "time to stop writing about bands." Besides, by then Gold was in demand as a food writer.

Over the years, Gold has written about food for California magazine (under the legendary Harold Hayes), the *LA Times* and Gourmet (both under Ruth Reichl). Despite a brief sojourn in New York for Gourmet, Gold has lived (and fressed) in Los Angeles for most his life, which puts Gold in a great position to discuss how the restaurant scene in Los Angeles became so vibrant, particularly as regards ethnic food. Gold attributes great importance to the 1984 LA Olympics. "There was a sense around the time of the Olympics in 1984 that suddenly Los Angeles was this international city," he says. "I don't think anyone had thought of it that way before."

Gold also believes the growth of California's ethnic cuisines are directly related to the global political events of the 1980s and 1990s: the wars in Central America which led substantial numbers of El Salvadorans, Ecuadorians, Hondurans, Guate-malans and Nicaraguans to make Los Angeles home; the fall of the shah in Iran, which led to the establishment of the Persian community here; and the concerns over Hong Kong coming under mainland control, which spurred a new wave of emigra-tion. Each new community brought its cooking with it, and new restaurants began to bloom.

At the same time, Los Angeles' Mexican restaurants, many of which were run by second-generation Americans, found themselves challenged by new establishments specializing in specific regional cooking. Beyond that, Los Angeles' Armenian, Thai and Korean restaurants continued to thrive, each offering their distinctive cuisines for Gold to sample on our behalf.

However, unlike other American cites, Los Angeles is so spread out and the communities are so insular that restaurants can serve the food of a particular region, or a particular city, for an audience that is almost entirely their own and never even have an English language menu.

"In LA's Koreatown," Gold gave as an example, a Korean restaurant "may never see a non-Korean customer."

How, you may wonder, can Gold even write about these various cuisines with any authority?

"I do my homework," he said. He owns more than 3,000 cookbooks, and he reads them. "By the time I write about a cuisine, I will have read most of what there is to read about it in English," he said.

"I don't go to a restaurant once, I go many times." The anecdote, which he has told several times since winning the Pulitzer, is of the Taiwanese restaurant that he hated, whose dishes he found repulsive, but that he kept going back to because he knew, in his words, that there was "intelligence at work in the kitchen."

As for his writing, Gold says: "Something that I've worked really, really hard at over the years [is] to be able to describe a dish [in a way] that makes you able to taste it."

Here's his description of the house-special crab at Macau Street restaurant in Monterey Park: "a plump, honestly sized crustacean dipped in thin batter, dusted with spices and fried to a glorious crackle, a pile of salty dismembered parts sprinkled with a handful of pulverized fried garlic and just enough chili slices to set your mouth aglow." Hungry yet? I'm willing to bet that even if you keep kosher, and never have and never will taste crab, you know what he means.

Gold also enjoys working pop culture references into his reviews "because food isn't the only world, it's part of the world, and I think one of the most important things is to put it into perspective. When I write about a place, I try almost every time ...to show where it might fit into your life."

Here's a recent example, from a review of A-Won restaurant in his recent "99 essential LA restaurants": "Good hwe dup bap—and A-won's is very good—is as alive and vivid and evanescent as a wildflower, the taste of the spring's first asparagus, or the throwaway line in a Lilly Allen song that breaks your heart."

Makes you wonder: Who's iPod is he playing?

Midway into our meal, we had done justice to the samsa, a puff pastry with ground meat—sort of a meat patty on steroids—that Gold judged to be "the bomb"; paid homage to the chuchvara, fried meat dumplings; had a degustation of an assortment of Tashkent-style salads; and had started to tuck into the plov.

As Gold remarked: "It's a grand thing to be a restaurant critic in the age of lipitor."

Gold is tall, with rock and roll long hair that was once blond (he could pass for the manager of the band in *Spinal Tap*)—and although he works out regularly, he would not be mistaken for an ironman competitor. Still, as he noted, given that his cholesterol is lower than it's ever been, "I'm still a fat guy. But I'm a healthier fat guy."

The Pulitzer was "completely unexpected," Gold says. "The Pulitzer traditionally goes to architecture writers and classical musical writers—you know: grown-ups." He is particularly happy for the recognition it brings to the *Weekly*. "My wife is the editor-in-chief and she works so hard, she puts out such great work…It's not like the family tailor shop, but it's mostly like the family tailor shop."

Asked to assess his contribution to Los Angeles, Gold says, "If I've done one thing in my twenty-five years, I hope I've let Angelenos know to not be quite so afraid of their neighborhoods—that you can drive to Bell Gardens and have a great meal and a great experience."

You might think that a meal with Gold is an exercise in excess or a CSI-type analysis of trace elements. But to the contrary, Gold is affable, friendly, relaxed. At lunch, he is not so much a food critic, as a restaurant enthusiast—he's just happy to be eating.

I asked Gold how he maintains his enthusiasm, given how long he's been reviewing restaurants. "It's strange," he admitted. "I still get excited every time I go into a new restaurant. I keep hoping that I'm going to have something that blows me away. Like today with this plov…" Gold's face lit up:

"The plov," he said, "is so good, really good."

July 12, 2007

BIG FUN UNDER THE BIG TOP

When I heard that the circus was coming to town, I couldn't wait to take my daughter. I'm talking about the Greatest Show on Earth, Ringling Bros. and Barnum & Bailey Circus, appearing in Orange County until August 5.

I know that Cirque du Soleil has its fans—but I find it too frou-frou, self-consciously artistic and pretentious, which may seem strange given all my own pretensions and affectations, but I can never make heads or tails of the incoherent pseudo-narratives of love and loss they thread through their shows. It may be impolitic to say so, but I go to the circus for the animal acts: the lions, tigers and elephants, even the acrobatic dogs. I still recall with pleasure seeing the famous dancing bears of The Moscow Circus. I remain a sucker for the high-wire acts, the trapeze, the human pyramids and, yes, the human cannonball, which still thrills me. This is what I was eager to share with my daughter.

During my childhood, Ringling Bros. made regular appearances at the old Madison Square Garden and we went often. My father loved parades and he loved the circus (I think his first girlfriend may have been a circus performer in Poland).

One highlight of my childhood was when I got to go "backstage." My best friend in second grade, Bill Doll Jr., had a father who was a legendary PR man, whose clients included Ringling Bros. We got to pet the elephants. I haven't seen or heard of Bill Doll in many decades, but I can't go to the circus without thinking of him.

Today, the Ringling Bros. and Barnum & Bailey Circus makes the "backstage" approach available to everyone in their free "All Access Pre-Show," where ticket holders can come down to the arena floor an hour before the show to meet and greet some of the performers, participate in juggling and face painting and watch the elephants paint their own works of art.

I had read that Ringling Bros. was getting rid of their three rings and adding a narrative to their shows to better compete with Cirque du Soleil as well as more intimate shows such as the Big Apple Circus—but that was not true of the show I attended at Staples Center.

This was the "Bellobration" show, which pivots around Bello the clown. Bello Nock, whose trademark blond hair stands on end, is part Harold Lloyd, part Pee-Wee Herman and is both acrobat and clown. Early in the show there was some attempt at a story line involving his affections for aerialist Erendira Wallenda, but that faded quickly, as the successive acts took hold in three-ring glory. Thank goodness.

The show itself has been modernized with the addition of a JumboTron, on which Bello appears in humorous prerecorded segments and which shows close-ups of the acts. Ty McFarlan, the ringmaster, has been less successfully updated: no top hat and no whip, and at one point he wore a costume that looked like he just came from a Star Wars convention—some things should hew to tradition.

Now for the animal acts: Cesar Milan would have no problem with the way Chilean Tabayara Antonio Maluenda de Campos (Taba) dominated his tigers, putting them through their paces in the caged ring. The white tigers on their hind legs were a fearsome sight. The Zotovas from Russia had dancing and prancing dogs, while the Olates from Chile had a fast-paced performance of acrobatic pooches who alternatively impressed and made you laugh; the Schwichtenbergs, Bulgarian natives, lead their Arabian, Fjord and Friesian horses and their zebras through paces that showcased their animals' beauty, grace and elegance. Finally, the elephants made several appearances, including a finale where they stood on their hind legs on platforms, their front legs resting on each other in a conga line of gargantuan proportions.

At this point, I should mention that animal rights activists have for some time targeted the circus—there were a handful of protesters outside the Staples Center. Ringling Bros. in no way avoided the issue; to the contrary throughout the show, in their programs and in all their public and press materials, they went to great length to discuss their animal care and preservation approach.

And now back to the show: In the air, we watched the flying Poemas, originally from Argentina, doing multiple somersaults; brothers Alberto and Mauricio Aguilar from Mexico performing great tricks on two parallel wires; Erendira on the sway pole, and her husband Nikolas Wallenda (son of the Flying Wallenda family) performing on "The Wheel of Steel," a Thunderdome-type contraption that spins like an amusement park ride, except that Wallenda is powering it by running on its outside.

Back on the ground, the Zunyi Troupe of Chinese contortionists assembled and reassembled themselves in mind-boggling human pyramids while the Ringling Bros. International Dancers—the circus' version of Rockettes or Lakers Girls—offered some glitz and eye candy for adults; the clowns performed a succession of routines throughout the program that my daughter enjoyed heartily (although I did miss the classic clown car and ambulance routines). The show's finale included Tina and Brian Miser of Peru, Ind., self-taught human cannonballs flying together out of a cannon Brian had custom made.

About now, you may be wondering, as my readers frequently do: What possible Jewish angle will there be to this column? Good question.

When I called Andy Perez, a Ringling Bros. spokesperson, to ask if there were any current Ringling Bros. performers who were Jewish or who came from Jewish circus families, he referred me to Jennifer Becker of Foundry Ink, his local publicist who was unable to locate any Jewish members of the show.

Perhaps Jewish circus performers have gone the way of Jewish boxers—a profession that flourished as part of an outsider, immigrant experience but that disappeared as Jews gained increased acceptance into white collar professional class and society in general. This is too bad, as Jews have a long history with the circus. The circus is generally thought to have started in Roman times ("pane et circum"), when Jews were free in Rome—but Jews avoided performing then whenever possible, as the original lion acts led to a high attrition rate among the human performers. In the Middle Ages, there was no formal circus but rather itinerant troupes of entertainers who often accepted Jews into their ranks. It was not until the nineteenth century in Europe that circuses as we know them today became popular—and Jews were often owners and performers. One of the most famous Jewish circus operators was Albert Solomon-sky, who founded the Nikulin Moscow Circus in 1880, which exists to this day. In 1888, he built the Riga Circus in Latvia, featuring the weight juggler Mifort Treyem (born Treyfem Meyer).

According to Marline Otte's *Jewish Identities in German Popular Entertainment, 1890-1933* (Cambridge, 2006), circuses provided Jewish performers and businessmen social mobility out of provincial ghettos, and many circuses came to rival leading theaters in their opulence. It was, in two simple words, "show business."

For many Europeans the circus represented a popular art rather than an elitist one. Its performers were regarded as artists, and some of its showmen were legendary.

William Breitbart, a prominent psychiatrist at Sloan-Kettering in New York, speaks proudly of his forebear the Polish circus strongman Siegmund (Zishe) Breitbart, known as "the modern Samson," and has even written an essay in an academic journal about visiting Zishe Breitbart's grave in the former East Berlin.

The Moscow Circus was so impressive that Lenin would come to hail the circus as one of the most important "arts" in revolutionary Russia (along with film).

In this country, carnivals and circuses attracted Jewish performers and entrepreneurs from both immigrant and established families. There was Paul Lewis (born Rosenberg) of the Lewis Bros. Circus in Michigan and Sy Rubens of Rogers Bros. Circus. Among circus performers, Abe Goldstein, who worked for Ringling Bros. and a number of other circuses, was regarded as "the Greatest Irish Cop Clown" in the business.

Finally, Ringling Bros. and Barnum & Bailey has its own Jewish history. Brothers Irvin and Israel Feld, who were more popularly known in their hometown of Hagerstown, Md., as Irv and Izzy, began their careers opening their Super-Cut Rate Drugstore in 1939. According to a 1954 *Time* magazine article, putting a record department in their store was such a success that it led them into the record business, and from there into the booking and concert business.

Beginning in 1957, The Felds were the booking agents for Ringling Bros. and in 1967, the Feld brothers purchased "The Greatest Show on Earth." In 1971, they sold it to Mattel, who struggled with the circus and their own financial problems, attempting at one point to sell it to Gulf Oil, before selling it back to the Feld Family in 1982. Since then it has remained in the Feld family, run by Kenneth Feld (Irvin's son), and Ken's daughter, Nicole Feld.

My research did turn up some important current Jewish circus performers of note, including foremost, Paul Binder, co-founder, ringmaster and artistic director of the Big Apple Circus. "Jews in the Circus," a 2003 article by Dan Pine from J.—the Jewish news weekly of Northern California, profiled the San Francisco Circus Center, mentioning current Jewish performers and owners such as aerialist and coach Jenn Cohen; Peggy Snider, co-founder of the Pickle Family Circus; as well as the Bronett family's Circus Scott in Sweden, once billed as "the most famous in Europe."

The circus delights and engages because it requires a suspension of disbelief—our normal expectations are confounded in a thousand ways—in a live show rather than on a flat screen that continues to amaze and delight "children of all ages."

For me then, history aside, it is wonderful to pass along a love for the circus from one generation to another. To that end, here is a report from my special correspondent, Natasha Teicholz, age nine:

I thought that the circus was absolutely the best show on earth. I'd give it a ten out of ten scale because it's funny. The sound effects were great and all the animals were amazing, mostly the tigers and the elephants. I can't wait to see the circus again with all of my friends.

Thank you, Daddy, for taking me to the circus!

July 26, 2007

ZSA ZSA GABOR: LAST OF THE

HUNGARIAN MOHICANS

"I want a man with kindness and understanding. Is that too much to ask of a millionaire?"—Zsa Zsa Gabor

Lately, I have been thinking about Zsa Zsa, and it makes me sad. A few years ago, she crashed her car on Sunset, and she has been wheelchair-bound since. She had been a recluse for some time before that, depressed, not wanting to leave the house. She, who for so long relied on her looks, no longer wants to be seen in public.

In recent weeks, Zsa Zsa has been in the news—albeit marginally so. Prince Frederic von Anhalt, her ninth husband, to whom she has been married since 1986, was recently found naked in his Rolls-Royce, bound and gagged. He claimed that three women he had stopped to help near the Bel Air Country Club had robbed him. The police are investigating.

A few weeks before that, the prince was in the news, claiming that he was the biological father of Anna Nicole Smith's baby and had been having a long-term affair with her. Not very nice to Zsa Zsa, particularly as the paternity suit did not go his way.

Two years ago, the prince and Zsa Zsa filed a lawsuit against her daughter, Francesca Hilton, charging, among other things, elder abuse, negligence and fraud, in a dispute over whether Francesca was entitled to certain monies relating to a Bel Air property. The lawsuit is ongoing.

Francesca is Zsa Zsa's only child, the daughter of her marriage to Conrad Hilton, the hotel chain magnate. Paris Hilton is Conrad's great-granddaughter.

One could characterize Zsa Zsa as the Paris of her day—someone famous for being famous, whose celebrity came more from her romantic entanglements, personal dramas and encounters with the police than from her professional accomplishments. However, to do so would ignore Zsa Zsa's intelligence, wit, charm and style. She was not glam—she was glamorous.

Sari (Zsa Zsa) Gabor was born February 6, 1917, in Budapest, the second of three daughters born to Vilmos Gabor and Janci Tilleman Gabor (known as Jolie). Magda was three years older, Eva two years younger.

Zsa Zsa and Eva were just a few years older than my mother, who knew them as girls whom she occasionally saw at the ice skating rink in Budapest. My mother used to say that she knew the Gabors so long ago, she knew them when they were Jewish. Zsa Zsa has acknowledged that her grandmother was Jewish—some sources say her father or his family converted to Catholicism—which was not uncommon for that generation of Hungarian Jews, who chose the religion more for the potential social advancement than as a question of faith.

And social advancement was very much Jolie's plan. Her mantra to her daughters being: "You will be rich, famous and married to kings."

During Zsa Zsa's teens, Jolie tried to launch her career by entering her in beauty contests—first in Budapest, then in Vienna. Although Zsa Zsa did not win, she landed a role in a Richard Tauber operetta and received enough attention when she got home that she had several suitors. She married a much older Turkish diplomat who took her off to Ankara, where Zsa Zsa made a great impression on the Turks (she was rumored to have had an affair with Kemal Ataturk, founder of the Turkish Republic).

By 1939, Eva was in Hollywood, launching her acting career. Magda, who had married an impoverished Polish count, remained in Budapest. During World War II, Magda became active in resistance activities as a driver for the International Red Cross. An affair with the Portuguese consul gave her access to false papers, which saved the lives of many, including her parents.

Zsa Zsa arrived in Los Angeles in 1941 on what was to be the first stop in a nationwide scout for a new husband. However, shortly after arriving, she was spotted at Ciro's by Hilton, a committed Catholic who had divorced his first wife but said he never intended to remarry.

Nevertheless, he fell under Zsa Zsa's spell and married her. She claimed that she, too, married for love (and at a much later date on a television show she passed a lie detector test when asked about it).

Still, the marriage only lasted five years. Hilton reportedly was tortured by the guilt of not being able to take communion and thwarted in his attempts to teach his wife thrift. Zsa Zsa was disappointed by Hilton's constant absences due to his business and the priority he placed on the hotels over her.

In 1946, at the time they began their highly public divorce proceedings, she was pregnant with their daughter, Francesca.

Shortly after Francesca's birth, Zsa Zsa experienced a bout of mania, characterized by volatile behavior, irrational spending splurges (even by Gabor standards) and dark, paralyzing depressions that led Eva to hospitalize her. Zsa Zsa was given insulin shock treatments. Upon her recovery, she turned on Eva, saying there was nothing wrong with her.

Zsa Zsa found her next husband in a movie theater, when she saw George Sanders on screen (she was reputed to have watched him beat a woman in *The Moon and Sixpence* only to remark, "That's the man for me!"). They were married in 1949. In 1951, Sanders won an Oscar for supporting actor for his role in *All About Eve*.

Around this time, Zsa Zsa's own career was launched when she appeared on the television show *Bachelor's Haven*, which allowed her to display her razor-sharp wit. When the host commented on her diamonds, Zsa Zsa retorted: "These? Darling, these are my working diamonds."

She became a regular on the program, as well as on radio. Often she would respond to listeners' questions. Here are some examples:

From a letter she read: "I'm breaking my engagement to a very wealthy man. He gave me a beautiful home, a mink coat, diamonds, an expensive car and a stove. What shall I do?" Zsa Zsa's advice: "You have to be fair, darling. Give back the stove."

Or: "My husband is a traveling salesman, but I know he strays even when he's at home. What should I do?"

Zsa Zsa's advice: "Shoot him in the legs."

Her sudden popularity led to her casting in "Lovely to Look At," by Hungarian-born producer Joe Pasternak, and perhaps her best role as Jane Avril in *Moulin Rouge,* directed by John Huston. Film roles followed in such films as *Lilli* (1953) and *Touch of Evil* (1958).

Although Sanders was the great love of Zsa Zsa's life, his interest in her waned—he was often away on location—so it was during that time that Zsa Zsa began an affair with legendary playboy Porfirio Rubirosa (she was the great love of his life). Scandal ensued as the couple's folie-a-deux had them fighting, making up and breaking up. At one point, Zsa Zsa appeared at a press conference with a patch over her eye, saying Rubirosa was a coward who beat women.

In the end, Zsa Zsa reconciled with Sanders, and Rubirosa married heiress Barbara Hutton. Rubirosa's marriage lasted all of seventy-three days. Sanders and Gabor divorced in 1954. However, Sanders was so enamored of the family and the family of him that in 1970, he married sister Magda (that one lasted six weeks).

What was the Gabors' appeal? First of all, as pictures from the era attest, they were beautiful (and they worked at being beautiful—one of Hilton's complaints was that it could take Zsa Zsa several hours to get ready to go out).

Zsa Zsa presented a new model of femininity to American audiences of the 1950s. She was the opposite of a bimbo, instead portraying herself as a worldly sophisticate not interested in traditional domestic life, a sexual being, a romantic and a pragmatist.

If Zsa Zsa could be characterized as a gold digger, the subtext to her image was that she was worth it. Zsa Zsa became a public character whom America enjoyed.

Eva was a more serious actress than her sister, appearing in such films as *A Royal Scandal* (1945), *The Last Time I Saw Paris* (1954) and *Don't Go Near the Water* (1957), and she is known to countless generations of children as the voices of Duchess in the animated film, *The Aristocats* and Bianca in *The Rescuers*.

Nonetheless, Eva achieved her greatest fame in the 1960s CBS sitcom, *Green Acres,* playing Eddie Albert's city-bred socialite wife, a role that, ironically, called on her to play a variation of Zsa Zsa, speaking in an exaggerated Hungarian accent (something she had worked to lose in her other roles). In the end, the Gabor girls created characters they could not escape.

For me, the Gabors were approximations of my mother and her friends—witty, attractive, entertaining women who got blonder every year, spoke in thick accents and loved jewelry (be it costume or real).

Several years ago, I tried to develop a movie about the Gabor girls—a story about these three ambitious, competitive women, their careers, their loves and their stage mother. As a framing device I thought to use the one occasion when all three sisters appeared on stage. In 1953, they performed at the Las Vegas Last Frontier Hotel in a show called, *The Gabors: This Is Our Life.* They appeared in beautiful sequined gowns, offered some witty lines and answered scripted questions. The show ran for only a few nights.

I never sold that project (or let's just say I haven't sold it yet), however, developing it led to one of my most memorable Hollywood moments: Lunch with Debbie Reynolds. What a trip, as they used to say.

Reynolds has been an actress since she was thirteen, and she is still (at that time she was almost seventy) every inch an actress. She had been a good friend of the Gabors, particularly Eva, and was interested in playing Jolie, the mother.

Actually, she was interested in playing all the parts, and at lunch, she easily slipped into Hungarian-accented English and showcased the variety of Gabor accents she could do. Also, perhaps because Reynolds achieved fame playing innocent in- génues such as Tammy and the Singing Nun, she delights in shocking.

At one point, I mentioned Zsa Zsa's appearance at the press conference wearing an eye patch because she claimed Rubi had given her a black eye. Reynolds didn't buy it: "She probably got a black eye falling on his 'rubirosa,'" (Reynolds didn't really say "rubirosa,"—she used a word that, although funny, is inappro- priate for a family-friendly newspaper.)

Over the last several decades, Zsa Zsa appeared in a wide variety of movies, from camp to trash, and in later years poked fun at herself but continued to be at her best as a talk show guest. Here are some more of her one-liners:

"Husbands are like fire. They go out when unattended."

"I am a marvelous housekeeper. Every time I leave a man, I keep his house."

"I believe in large families: Every woman should have at least three husbands."

"I wasn't born, I was ordered from room service."

Although famous, Zsa Zsa attained notoriety in 1989 when she went on trial for slapping a Beverly Hills police officer—it was not the first time she had behaved poorly—just the first time she crossed the line with an officer of the court. She re- ceived a sentence of three days in jail—and plenty of publicity.

Finally, it should be noted that the Gabors were all success- ful businesswomen. Magda at one point ran a thriving plumbing business for many years, Eva had a wig business, Zsa Zsa made personal appearances for the Marshall Field's department store and even Mama Jolie had a successful costume jewelry store on Madison Avenue in New York. The facts of their lives have been told often, by the Gabors themselves. Jolie published two books (the eponymous *Jolie Gabor* by gossip doyenne Cindy Adams and *Jolie Gabor's Family Cookbook* by Ted and Jean Kaufman). Zsa Zsa wrote four (*Zsa Zsa Gabor: My Story Written for Me by Gerold Frank, How to Catch a Man, How to Keep a Man, How to Get Rid of a Man, It's Simple Darling* and *One Lifetime Is Not Enough,* assisted by, edited by and put into proper English by Wendy Leigh). Eva wrote one *(Orchids and Salami: A Gay and Impudent Memoir).*

Others have tackled the subject in articles in newspapers and magazines, on television and in books. As recently as 2001, Anthony Tutu published his collection of Gabor artifacts in *Gaborabilia,* a tribute book written with Donald F. Reuter.

Nonetheless, and this is what makes me sad, it seems as though their time has passed.

Eva died in 1995, Mama Jolie in 1997 (she was 103), Magda a few weeks later the same year. This past February, Zsa Zsa turned ninety.

Having outlived her sisters, perhaps Zsa Zsa is the last of the blonde-haired, bejeweled Hungarian Mohicans. In her Beverly Hills home, I trust that she feels she is not entirely alone or forgotten.

Perhaps there is some measure of pleasure for her in the fact that despite her current problems, she is still remembered for her beauty and her wit. She can, if she likes, consider this column a gift from a perfect stranger. But I will give Zsa Zsa the last word:

"I don't accept gifts from perfect strangers—but then nobody's perfect."

August 23, 2007

SUMMER AND THE START OF SCHOOL

In one of his most famous works, the French poet Francois Villon asked: "Mais ou sont les neiges d'antan? (But where are the snows of yesteryear?)." I might ask the same about where this summer went. It seems like just last week my daughter was getting out of class, and now she's about to start up again. This year, summer just slipped through my fingers.

Americans are often chided for their inability to go on vacation—a problem I've never had, but this year work beckoned louder. I don't think I was alone. Given the volatility in the stock, real estate and mortgage markets, and the potential of a strike in Hollywood, it seemed to me like fewer people I know took lengthy vacations.

My summer idyll was but a few days in Laguna. However, it made me think about those qualities that define a summer. If I close my eyes to conjure up the spirit of summers past, here's what comes to mind:

Sleepaway summer camp, which was all about summer friends and another chance to be the person you wanted to be, unfettered by how you were defined at school. It was about trying new sports, and progressing in others (like finally getting up on the mono water ski); it was about peer education on a multitude of subjects including, but not limited to, sex education (both theoretical and applied); it was about a world without parents, where the authority figures (the counselors) were not yet adults themselves (although we thought they were).

Summers were also about travel and being on a beach. My parents were big proponents of traveling to places in "the off season" and of staying in the worst room at the best hotel. It was a strategy that sometimes backfired (summering in Miami), and occasionally succeeded (a very strange room at the very wonderful Carlton Hotel in Cannes).

Each summer, it seemed, had its book, its movie, its song. For me, summer reading (as opposed to required reading) was the alternative education that took place outside of school. Dog-eared copies of books passed from friend to friend and traveler to traveler such as *Siddhartha* (Hermann Hesse), *Children of the Albatross* (Anais Nin), *The Dharma Bums* (Jack Kerouac), *Cat's Cradle* (Kurt Vonnegut), *Still Life With Woodpecker* (Tom Robbins), *Snow Crash* (Neal Stephenson) and *Tapping the Source* (Kem Nunn).

Jaws became the prototype for the summer movie, creating a monster that today exists independent of the taste of most adults. While the summer song was a pop confection that has traveled from rock (The Doors' "Light my Fire"; The Stones' "Some Girls") to pure pop (Katrina and the Waves' "Walking on Sunshine") to increasingly suggestive or explicit slow raps (Kelis' "Milkshake").

Although *The New York Times* anointed Rihanna's "Umbrella" as this summer's tune, it was not for me (not Rihanna's version, nor Mandy Moore's cover). Instead, I found myself listening to Avril Lavigne's "Girlfriend," when my daughter was in the car, and Amy Winehouse's "Rehab" when she wasn't. At the movies, this summer belonged to Judd Apatow and Seth Rogan. In *Knocked Up* and *Superbad,* they found a way to toggle among honesty, absurdity and vulgarity in a most entertaining way. As for books, I confess to being in a bit of a rut. I read little for pleasure, and what I read didn't grab me.

This summer I watched a lot of cable—there were a lot of shows to TiVo, including *Damages* and *State of Grace* for the performances of, respectively, Glenn Close and Holly Hunter; such guilty pleasures as *Burn Notice* and *Hotel Babylon,* and such old but still good shows as *The Closer, Monk, Entourage* and, more recently, *Weeds* to remark on how good it is or *Californication* to talk about how bad it is (can someone find me an agent who lines up paying gigs blogging?—even if it's a setup).

This may also be remembered as the summer of the iPhone—which I say not as an indictment of entertainment but surely a sign that the technology is becoming more important than the product, or the product more important than the content.

For me, this summer was also about learning new things about the Internet and gaining a deeper understanding of online ventures—I learned new (to me) words such as wireframes, folksonomy and tag clouds (go ahead, look them up). I discovered the strange worlds of twitter, twittervision and yurth.com, and began to sense that Google Earth was becoming as important an organizing principle to information on Internet pages as the shuffle feature had become to music.

And so back to school. With slight trepidation, the new year stands before us, calling us to dive in and embrace the fall.

One of the great movies of my youth was *Endless Summer,* a surf documentary whose title embraced the dream that summer could go on and on (if only). This year, I didn't stop for summer, I kept keeping on. What I missed was not a book or a movie or a song, but a feeling as inchoate as the sand between your toes or a warm breeze at night—a feeling that is already gone.

September 8, 2007

LET US TRAVEL TO IRAN

This fall, I am asking you to travel to Iran. Not the present-day, front-page, headline-grabbing, nuclear-developing, Holocaust-denying, Israel-hating Iran, but the Iran of just twenty or thirty years ago, as described in two newly published novels, Gina Nahai's *Caspian Rain* (MacAdam Cage) and Dalia Sofer's *The Septembers of Shiraz* (Ecco).

Although Nahai's novel takes place over the decade leading up to the 1979 Iranian revolution and Sofer's in the years immediately following it, both are beautifully written, absorbing and moving accounts of life in Tehran. Both concern Jewish families and tell their stories by alternating chapters among family members.

Although two novels do not a trend make, that won't stop me from declaring one: The Persian Jewish novel has come of age.

In *Caspian Rain*, Nahai tells the story of Omid and his wife, Bahar. She is from a poor observant family; he's from a wealthy assimilated one. Although ostensibly narrated by Yaas, their young daughter, Nahai lets us enter each character's world and uses the specifics of their lives, the details of their class differences, their social standing as Jews in Iran and within the Jewish community itself, as well as the pressures from their in-laws, Yaas' school and Muslim society to render an emotionally complex portrait of a couple imprisoned each in their own way by marriage and family. But it is also Yaas' story, as she has a secret all her own, trying to make sense of it all.

At this point, although I don't want to give away any important plot points, let me reveal that I know Nahai. We served together on the board of the writer's organization, PEN Center USA. She is also a monthly columnist for this newspaper. However, those are just two of Nahai's impressive credentials.

Nahai was born in Iran and holds a master's degree in international relations from UCLA and a master of fine arts in writing from USC, where she currently teaches creative writing. She has consulted for the Rand Corp. and done research for the U.S. Department of Defense.

More to the point, *Caspian Rain* is Nahai's fourth novel. Her first, *Cry of the Peacock,* (Crown, 1991), according to Nahai's own Web site, "told for the first time in any Western language the 3,000-year story of the Jews in Iran." Her second novel, *Moonlight on the Avenue of Faith,* was nominated for England's Orange Prize, and the third, *Sunday's Silence,* charts the intersecting lives of an Iranian Jew and a Christian fundamentalist in North Carolina.

Nahai's curriculum vitae, however, does not prepare one for the magical, dreamlike quality of her prose in *Caspian Rain.* She does a beautiful job of ushering us through an Iran most of us don't know—of colors and scents, of mountains and beaches, of slums and mansions. Her novel is filled with eccentric characters, including a bicycle-riding ghost brother, but it is the poetry and the emotional quality of Nahai's writing that will linger long after the book is closed.

By contrast, if Nahai writes of Iran in the most subjective of tones, Sofer, in *The Septembers of Shiraz,* has brought a hard-edged focus to her description—making objective details of her characters' experiences so real as to deliver insight not only into the Iran that was but in the Iran that has now come to be.

Sofer was also born in Iran, just before the revolution, and she fled with her family to the United States at the age of 10. She has a master of fine arts degree in creative writing from Sarah Lawrence, and this, her first novel, makes her accomplishment all the more impressive.

Sofer's story begins with the arrest of Isaac Amin, a wealthy Jewish gem dealer, by Iran's Revolutionary Guard. Being Jewish, he is suspected of being an Israeli spy; being wealthy, he is accused of having become so at the expense of the Iranian people.

His wife, Farnaz, tries to find out where he is being held and struggles to find a way to help him, even as her housekeeper turns on her, and her housekeeper's son loots their home and office.

Their young daughter is in class with the daughter of a Revolutionary Guard member and attempts to launch her own counterrevolution. Parviz, their son, is in New York studying to be an architect, but he is lonely and cut off and lives in the Brooklyn basement of a Chasidic family.

Sofer's tale provides insight into the anger of the Iranian revolutionaries and those who supported them, as well as how they justified their behavior to those they deemed their enemies.

On one level, Sofer's story would be no less powerful if it were set in Prague (think Kafka's *The Trial*) or in Argentina

(Timmerman's memoir, *Prisoner Without a Name, Cell Without a Number,* comes to mind), but the nuances of Jewish life in Iran and of post-revolutionary Iran make the story distinctive and memorable. It is different, yet strangely familiar.

In recent years, there has been an explosion of memoirs, novels and even graphic comics about Iran. More recently, there has been an effort to collect the stories of Persian Jews, including through the establishment in Los Angeles of a Center for Iranian Jewish Oral History and the publication in English of Houman Sarshar's *Esther's Children: A Portrait of Iranian Jews.*

Why Iran? Why now, you may ask.

In part, it is incredible that such an old and established Jewish community is unknown to most of us, and that the life they led is, for the most part, no more.

Although Jews were reported to have lived in what is now Iran as early as the eighth century B.C.E., most accounts of Jewish life in Persia begin in 597 B.C.E., following Chaldean King Nebuchadnezzar's conquest of Judea. At that time, the First Temple in Jerusalem was ransacked, and 10,000 Jewish captives were taken to Babylon—so when Bob Marley sings "by the rivers of Babylon" and weeps "for he remembers Zion," he is singing the song of Jewish exile.

Less than sixty years later, when the Persian king, Cyrus, conquered Babylon, he gave the Jews the right to practice their religion and to return to Jerusalem to build the Second Temple. Many Jews decided, however, to remain in what is now Iran. For the next several centuries, the Jewish community in Persia flourished. The biblical books of Jeremiah, Ezra, Daniel and, of course, Esther (the Purim story), all make reference to the Jews of Persia. Scholars recorded the oral law in the form of the Babylonian Talmud—a text studied to this day. Jewish poets, scholars, philosophers all made their home in Persia.

Beginning in the second century, as Zoroastrianism grew in popularity, minority groups in Persia, including the Jews, suffered attacks and prejudice. However, it was the conquest of Iran by Islam in the seventh century, when Jews and other non-Muslims became second-class citizens called "dhimmis" and were forced to pay a special tax. Over the next millennia, the fate of Persia's Jews waxed and waned, suffering massacres, forced conversions or persecutions under certain rulers, while being given greater freedom by others.

In 1925, conditions changed substantially for the Jews with the advent of the Pahlavi regime, under Reza Shah. Non-Muslims were no longer considered "unclean," and he abolished the restrictions on Jews, such as the ghetto. Nonetheless, anti-Semitism flared occasionally, particularly at such moments as when Iran sided with the Nazis and at the time of the founding of the State of Israel.

In 1941, Reza Shah was forced to abdicate, following an Anglo-Soviet invasion of Iran. Nonetheless, his son, Mohammed Reza Pahlavi succeeded him as shah and by 1953 consolidated his power. He launched a series of actions to modernize Iran, while at the same time increasing his power and repressing dissent.

The shah's regime was an era of unparalleled freedom and prosperity for Iran's Jews as they rose to positions of prominence in many fields.

Under the shah, Jews came to believe, as they have in every society where they have been allowed to be free, that they were Iranians, same as everyone else. History proved otherwise.

With the benefit of hindsight, the experience of the successful, wealthy, assimilated Jewish Iranians of the 1960s and seventies was a rare historical moment. Their rise in Persian society throughout the Pahlavi dynasty—from the slums and ghetto of south Tehran to the highest ranks of society—could be seen as comparable and as rare as that of the Jews in Vienna around 1900, in Berlin in the 1920s or Budapest or Warsaw in the 1930s. Those eras were not paradise for all Jews, but they now seem fleeting memories, nonetheless.

The shah was deposed in 1979. It is estimated that eighty-five percent of Iran's Jewish population has fled the country since then. There are today more Iranian Jews in Los Angeles (approximately 35,000) than there are in Tehran (an estimated 25,000).

The Persian community are double exiles—forever contained in their exile first to Babylon and then from Iran. Perhaps that is part of why they are so special.

Living in Los Angeles, as I do, one of the added benefits has been getting to know members of the Persian Jewish community, as well as being exposed to Persian culture and cuisine (Javan is on our speed dial for home delivery).

Los Angeles and Beverly Hills have their share of wealthy Persian Jewish families living in a world some have dubbed "Tehrangeles."

A few years ago, my wife and I were invited to a party at a Persian home (where the husband, coincidentally, is a successful gem dealer). The party was called for 10 p.m. Most guests didn't show up before 11:00 p.m., and when they did, there was wonderful food served on large platters, with even more amazing sweet desserts and mint tea.

The men were all in suits, the women were all dressed elegantly, coiffed, in makeup and wearing serious jewels. The dance floor was crowded; there was a disco ball and a DJ playing dance hits sung in Persian.

Among the couples I spoke with, I found a great warmth and a certain detachment, which I understood. This is the language of exile; these are the immigrants and the immigrants' children, the first and second generations, who have come from an older culture to one that at times finds them foreign.

One other thing: The displays of wealth—the enjoyment of wealth—which is sometimes seen among Persian Jews is something that I recognize, as well. It is no different from the way the wealthy German Jewish families I knew in New York pretended to take their wealth for granted or the affection of Hungarian Jews for chandeliers in their homes.

To me, this is just a secular form of "hidur mitzvah," which roughly translates to beautifying the deed—the Judaic Martha Stewart-like concept that beauty in presentation enhances the ritual—that, for example, ornate tabernacles, well-decorated sukkahs, a beautifully set table, even dressing well for synagogue, are all pleasing to God.

Which brings me back to the Persian Jewish novel.

Its time has come because writers, as well as readers, are always looking to reclaim the world that is no longer. From the last century, one thinks of Stefan Sweig writing about Vienna or Joseph Roth writing about Berlin in the 1920s or Giorgio Bassani writing about the *Garden of the Finzi Continis* (Sofer did a segment for NPR's *All Things Considered* and talked about how well she relates to that novel). Zweig called his memoir, *The World of Yesterday,* and there is always the compulsion to record how it was, particularly when world history convulses personal history.

Beyond that, when a writer asks him or herself that crucial series of questions: What is mine? What is the story I know better than others? What is the best story I know, what territory or landscape is mine and not others? What is unique?—they often find themselves drawn back to their childhoods or, as Irving Howe put it, the "world of our fathers." By revisiting the lost world, novelists try to re-create and reimagine those worlds, to let others know what happened, to explain it to others and perhaps to themselves, and in so doing, they arrive at a greater truth in the telling.

Both Nahai and Sofer lead us to a Tehran that no longer exists. Yet neither work is an exercise in nostalgia.

Nahai's *Caspian Rain* lets us experience the conflicts of lives before the revolution, while Sofer's *The Septembers of Shiraz* illuminates the moment (always too late) when we realize how change will affects us.

The specificity of the Iranian Jewish experience deepens the characters, rendering them more credible, and, because we understand the choices before them, it makes these novels more universal in their appeal. If that doesn't seem logical, consider the worldwide popularity of Isaac Bashevis Singer's stories.

So let us travel to Iran. With Nahai and Sofer to guide us, we can still experience the drama, the conflicts and the pleasures of a lost world.

September 20, 2007

RIVERS OF MUSIC

Producer, songwriter and musician Larry Klein is having a good year. In a way, one could say his current success is the culmination of a process of recontextualizing his background, his experience, his talents and his interests.

Two records he produced have just been released on Verve Records: *River: The Joni Letters* by jazz great Herbie Hancock, an exploration of the songs of Joni Mitchell (who is Klein's ex-wife); and *The New Bossa Nova* by Brazilian-born singer and composer Luciana Souza (his new wife). Starbucks has just released Joni Mitchell's new album, *Shine,* on which he plays, and he's been co-writing and producing a new record by Walter Becker of Steely Dan fame.

Recently, over lunch at Hal's in Venice, Klein recounted that when Verve first brought up the idea of working on *The Joni Letters* with Hancock, his reaction was "what a great way to bind together a number of different threads." The theme of weaving together his various talents and interests—professional and personal—is a neat way to encapsulate Klein's professional journey.

Klein grew up, he recalled, "in an area of Los Angeles that is now known for its Chinese food, Monterey Park." His parents say it had a sizeable Jewish community when they first moved there, but that was not the case when he was growing up. "By the time I was five or six, there were few Jewish families and a healthy [or unhealthy] dose of anti-Semitism," he said.

Music and literature proved his salvation. They were, he says, "my escape." Initially inspired by his parents' record collection, Klein began his musical education by taking guitar lessons at a "typical suburban music store," where the teacher sometimes fell asleep during the lesson.

However, in junior high school his mother enrolled him in The Community School for the Performing Arts, an after-school music program, sponsored by USC, which allowed him to take classes in composition and music theory. At Schnurr High School he was also fortunate to have a "Mr. Holland"-type teacher in Wayne Bischoff.

"He was an incredible character and introduced me to so much music—Charles Ives, [and] the entire history of classical music." As a result, Klein spent about three quarters of his day studying music. He also spent time outside of class going to concerts and seeing such legends as Jimi Hendrix and early performances by James Taylor and Jackson Browne.

Klein started playing in rock bands in sixth grade. He switched to bass early on. Rock, however, was only a small part of the wide swath of music that interested him. "I was a maniacal fan of Charles Ives," Klein recalled. "I got into serial composition and would listen to a lot of Schoenberg and Anton Weber."

As Klein got serious about playing bass, he also became more interested in jazz. "There were only a certain amount of challenges available to a bass player in the rock genre."

By age seventeen, Klein was playing professionally around Los Angeles with Latin percussionist Willie Bobo, including at places like The Comeback Inn on Abbott Kinney in Venice. "This was a great place to meet some of the most exciting musical talents, such as drummer Chester Thompson (who played with Frank Zappa and with Genesis), and jazz pianist George Cables." It was there that jazz trumpeter Freddie Hubbard heard Klein and offered him a job on the road with him. Although Klein had graduated high school early and was enrolled in Cal State LA as a music major, he took the offer.

"That was my master class," Klein said, "as Freddie was fond of pointing out."

He was living his dream as a jazz bassist and playing with his heroes, and there was a large market for rock-inflected jazz at the time—Miles Davis had led the way, and others, including Hubbard, were experimenting and playing large concert halls.

Nonetheless, after five years with Hubbard, at times spending eight months of the year on the road, Klein had had enough. Gradually he'd become "impatient with the narrowness of that world."

He decided to work on his songwriting and do more studio work. However, being a studio musician meant playing a lot of record dates for music that he neither loved, nor even liked.

"A lot of the music didn't feel honest or inspiring," Klein recalled, "I became frustrated with that role."

Around that time, he got a call to work on a Joni Mitchell album, *Wild Things Run Fast*. The album, which came out in 1982, took a year to record and carried the following credit: "Special thanks to Larry Klein for caring about and fussing over this record with me." Over the year a friendship had developed into a love affair, and they married in November 1982.

Klein began a personal and creative collaboration with Mitchell that involved producing, writing and playing on her albums, including *Dog Eat Dog, Chalk Mark in a Rainstorm, Night Ride Home* and *Turbulent Indigo.*

So, I asked him: What was it like to write with Joni Mitchell?

"With her it was a very simple process," Klein said. "Basically, I was always writing music, and she would hear something through the wall that she liked, and she would say, 'Give me that.'"

At the same time, Klein was moving into solo producing. "I wanted to find a new way to integrate everything I knew." In 1986, he produced *The Lace,* a solo album for Benjamin Orr of The Cars. Over the next decade, he also produced albums by Shawn Colvin, Holly Cole and Julia Fordham. More recently he has produced albums by Rebecca Pidgeon (*Tough on Crime*) and Madeleine Peyroux (*Careless Love*).

Klein describes the late 1980s and nineties as a time when he was "crop rotating" between songwriting, production and playing. The variety of assignments allowed him to be pickier about whom he played for—and, as a result, he performed with, as he put it, "people who were my heroes." He played on the soundtrack to *Raging Bull* with Robbie Robertson, which led to playing on Robertson's solo album, as well as with Don Henley on all his solo records. He also played with Tracy Chapman, Aaron Neville, Bryan Adams and wrote songs with Bonnie Raitt and Warren Zevon.

Doing so also allowed him to learn from other producers, such as Robert John "Mutt" Lang, who has produced and/or written massive hits for AC/DC, Foreigner, The Cars, Bryan Adams, and Shania Twain (to whom Lang is married). Klein credits Lang with being "incredibly talented at making the complex sound simple." However, more than anyone, Klein credits Mitchell with teaching him the most important parts of producing: "How to say what, when" (which Klein admits he sometimes learned the hard way); and "how to adeptly bring out the best in an artist that they can possibly put forward at a given juncture in their career and artistic development."

Although Klein and Mitchell divorced in 1994, they have continued to work together—and the current projects are evidence of that.

The idea behind *River: The Joni Letters,* Klein says, was that "we wanted the entire record to emanate from the poetry." Klein and Hancock spent two months on preproduction, winnowing down a list of songs, talking about the lyrics, and discussing the best singers for the songs, who came to include Norah Jones, Corinne Bailey Rae, Souza and Tina Turner (who, as far as I am concerned is the big surprise here, turning in a vocal performance that recalls Ella Fitzgerald), along with a reading by Leonard Cohen that Hancock improvises around. The recording also includes Mitchell singing on "Tea Leaf Prophecy," a song she wrote with Klein about her parents' courtship.

Several of the tracks are instrumental, and in these, as in all the tracks, Klein and Hancock sought to "get away from conventional Jazz structure," which Klein characterized as "melody, solo, solo, solo, play the melody and out."

"We approached this more as a dialogue," Klein told me. The album, Klein explained, is "geared toward Joni's world" and includes two songs not written by Mitchell but "that were important songs in her musical development."

One is *Solitude,* by Duke Ellington, which Mitchell first heard as a nine-year-old. As sung by Billie Holiday, "it kind of set off something inside her." The other is *Nefertiti,* by Wayne Shorter; Mitchell heard Miles Davis' version, Klein said, and "it's one of those records that knocks you on your ass, and you think, 'Wow!'"

Klein sees Souza's *The New Bossa Nova* as a companion piece to the Hancock recording: "Both records come from the same germ." He believes that as listeners, we get inured to the lyrics in great songs, and that setting them in a new musical context—"recontextualizing them"—makes us appreciate the lyrics anew.

So Klein and Hancock turned to jazz for Mitchell, and Klein and Souza looked to 1960s bossa nova style to recast the songs of such great contemporary American songwriters as Sting, Brian Wilson and James Taylor (who duets with Souza on his song *Never Die Young"*). Souza also bridges the span between Brazil and America with a gorgeous English language version of Jobim's gem *The Waters of March.*

Klein and Souza just celebrated their first wedding anniversary. They met when Souza, who is the daughter of Brazilian songwriters Walter Santos and Teresa Souza, performed as a soloist at Walt Disney Hall in a piece written by Billy Childs, one of Klein's former classmates from The Community School program. They were married here in Los Angeles by Rabbi Mordecai Finley. Souza, who became a Jew-by-choice under Finley's tutelage, gives the following credit on her album: "To Mordecai Finley, for the beacon."

At which point Klein offered up the story of his own spiritual journey. "I went to Hebrew school and got bar mitzvahed, and after getting bar mitzvahed, I could not get away fast enough," he replied.

Although Klein describes himself as being of "a spiritual bent" and "spiritually curious," he found that the Judaism he was taught was "so by rote and so devoid of any pragmatic application or real etymological tying-in to how these ideas should be interpreted, that I could see nothing about it that was interesting." Instead he became interested in Buddhism, which he studied for many years.

"I was most interested in Tibetan Buddhism, but never found a community in that tradition that felt really honestly viable for me," he said.

Several years ago, while working with Rebecca Pidgeon on her album, over the course of many philosophical discussions she suggested to Klein that he might attend a Sabbath service with her and her husband, David Mamet, at Ohr HaTorah, with Finley.

"I was just astounded," Klein says. In Finley, Klein found "someone teaching who really understood the philosophical implications of the Torah and also the metaphoric subtleties. The way that Finley spoke of Judaism and Torah was, in Klein's words, "a whole new thing for me." After a few more visits, Klein went to Ohr HaTorah for the High Holy Days.

"I thought, 'Wow!'" Klein recalled, "Isn't it ironic that this is what I was looking for?"

As I said earlier, recontextualizing has been very, very good for Klein. And for all of us, the beneficiaries of *The Joni Letters*, *The New Bossa Nova*, and all the rivers of music that Klein has to share.

October 11, 2007

ADVENTURES OF TOM & CHABON

Novelist Michael Chabon has an agent, Steven Barclay, who handles his speaking engagements and who scheduled my interview with Chabon for 8:15 a.m. on the morning of Halloween. When I asked Barclay what self-respecting writer does interviews at 8:15 a.m., he said: "A very busy one."

Point well taken.

Chabon, whose first novel, *The Mysteries of Pittsburgh*, was written as his master's thesis at UC Irvine, and who currently lives in Berkeley with his wife, writer Ayelet Waldman, and their four kids, will come to Los Angeles on Sunday, November 11, as part of the inaugural Celebration of Jewish Books at American Jewish University (formerly the University of Judaism).

Chabon's novels also include *Wonder Boys* (which became a Curtis Hanson film with Michael Douglas and Tobey Maguire), as well as the Pultizer Prize-winning *The Amazing Adventures of Kavalier & Clay*, which tells the story of a comic-creating duo set in the 1930s and forties, during the golden age of comics and, not coincidentally, the time of the Holocaust. His recent works include *The Yiddish Policeman's Union*, a murder mystery that imagines an alternative history, in which after a failed creation of the State of Israel, many Jews create a homeland in Alaska, and the just-published *Gentlemen of the Road,* a swashbuckling epic of tenth century Khazari Jews in Central Asia, which Chabon originally wanted to title, *Jews With Swords.*

Chabon is that rare writer who can provide delight in his embrace of culture both high and low, and whose work is enjoyed for the beauty of his sentences, the wordplay he engages in and the ambition of his novels. At the same time, although his novels consistently feature Jewish characters, he is rarely characterized as a "Jewish" novelist. Given his appearance at the Celebration of Jewish Books, I set out to discuss the Jewish nature of his work. The following conversation has been edited for narrative coherence (words in brackets are mine, not Chabon's).

Tom Teicholz: Sometimes when I read the questions I'm going to ask, such as, 'So what it is with you and the Jews?' I feel like I'm writing for Der Sturmer instead of The Jewish Journal. But that is my first question. Your books seem to be getting increasingly more Jewish or more filled with Jewish characters.

Michael Chabon: That's a good way of putting it.

TT: Do you notice this as well? Is it conscious? Does it have anything to do with raising four kids?

MC: I think the answer is 'yes' to all of those questions. It's both conscious—certainly I notice it—it is both conscious and unconscious.

TT: Are you surprised by it?

MC: Not anymore. It feels very natural and inevitable. I definitely crept in through the back door in terms of including Jewish characters and Jewish themes and subject matter in my work. It was always present. If you go back and you look at my first book [*The Mysteries of Pittsburgh*], you can see it there, as well; the gangsters in my first novel are Jewish gangsters.

But in terms of being not only conscious but subconscious about it, I think that is a development that's probably tied in ways I don't even understand to the experience of having children and making a family and finding a way of creating a Jewish home that felt honest and comfortable and true to me and to my wife, but that also felt meaningful and authentic.

TT: I find that living in California is very much about trying and being able to create your own way.

MC: Absolutely, I agree completely.

TT: It applies to Judaism, and it applies to you—you are someone who is creating your own worlds in your books.

MC: Yes, definitely. We just came through the experience on Saturday—my oldest child, my daughter, Sophie, had her bat mitzvah.

TT: Gosh—mazel tov.

MC: Thank you. It was wonderful. And we very much did it ourselves. It was an independent bat mitzvah. She studied independently with a teacher, a lay teacher, who then led the service, along with my daughter; my sister-in-law, who's a cantor, sang, and I made the siddur myself.

So we're definitely part of that overall experience (and certainly not just by any means Jewish experience) [that is] part of the California ethos to find your own way to do things—whether it's spiritual things or creative things or putting Thai barbecue chicken on a pizza.

TT: Your subject matter has gone from Jewish gangsters and gay protagonists (*The Mysteries of Pittsburgh*) to drunken pot-smoking, failed novelists (*Wonder Boys*) to comic books (*The Amazing Adventures of Kavalier & Clay*) to Yiddish policemen (*The Yiddish Policemen's Union*) and now Jews with swords (*Gentlemen of the Road*). It almost seems as if you're tempting fate to find what would be by definition a less commercial subject and then make it charming.

MC: I guess the best way to explain it is I have a lot of ideas and a lot of different things occur to me in the course of my working life. Certain ideas just seem to lodge in my brain. I find myself thinking about them for so long that I finally realize that the reason I keep thinking about them is that I'm meant to write about it. At that point, I just go for it, and I don't give any thought at all to who's going to want to read this or is there anyone actually interested in this subject at all besides me.

In the case of the latest one, it sort of all came to me at once one day when I took my kids to the Santa Cruz Beach boardwalk, and I had my notebook with me. I spent the day waiting while they rode on the rides—sitting on benches and taking notes for this strange adventure story set among the Khazars.

After that day was over, I put the notebook away, and I had other things I needed to do. I kept thinking about those two guys, and when *The New York Times* called and offered me a chance to write a serialized novel about three years later, the first thing that popped into my mind were the notes I had taken that summer day three years before. And I found this desire to do it was just as intense as it was that day.

TT: How did you stumble into the Khazars?

MC: I just must have read about it. I was always interested in Jewish history, generally. As a kid, I had books of strange and surprising facts from Jewish history. I think most Jews are interested in the subject of the lost Jews of history and various surprising groups of Jews: The mountain Jews of Central Asia and the Chinese Jews of Kaifeng and the Jews of India and African Jews, and all those odd pockets of the world where you find Jews.

That's a perennial subject of fascination and has been, going back to the Khazars themselves. I just shared in the greater fascination that Jews tend to have for these strange lost races of Jews throughout time.

November 8, 2008

LA'S PHOTO LAUREATE

Julius Shulman

Julius Shulman, the still much-in-demand architectural photographer, famous for his photos of Modernist homes, turned ninety-seven a few weeks ago, and the partying has been pretty much nonstop—which is the way Shulman likes it.

The Getty Research Institute, which houses Shulman's photographic archive of more than 260,000 negatives, prints and transparencies, organized *Shulman's Los Angeles,* an exhibition of 150 of Shulman's photographs, spanning his seventy-year-career, which is currently on view at downtown's Central Public Library through January 20.

The show gives a great sense not only of how Los Angeles grew but of Shulman's role in its maturation, as Christopher James Alexander, Getty associate curator for architecture, said, "as Los Angeles' No. 1 fan." Organized into several narratives that document the development and expansion of Los Angeles, such as *Downtown and the Rise of Bunker Hill, Century City: Downtown Moves West* and *Wilshire Boulevard: An Axis in Evolution,* the exhibition also includes a section called, "Only in

LA," of iconic buildings, ranging from the Watts Towers, to the Academy Theater, Grauman's Chinese Theatre and Johnny's Restaurant.

Shortly before the exhibition opened, I visited Shulman at his home atop Woodrow Wilson Drive in the Hollywood Hills. We had made an appointment for 10 a.m., but my on-time arrival woke up Shulman.

"I had a late night," he said by way of excuse. Dressed in a royal-blue bathrobe, he led me to a seating area in his living room, where for the next two and a half hours, interrupted by the occasional phone call about arrangements for a party he was attending that night, Shulman regaled me with the story of his life—thus far.

What was most evident throughout our conversation was Shulman's continued air of delight. Despite his age, his more than seventy-year professional career, all the honors, accolades and all the times he has told his story to reporters, students, curators, academics and fans, Shulman appears gobsmacked by his good fortune, his success, even by his own talent. He continues to appreciate and be amazed by his photos, by his compositions, which express glamour and visceral beauty, while capturing an organic natural order to the buildings he photographs.

Shulman repeatedly emphasized how he had no ambition, no training. He also repeatedly expressed the pleasure he derives just from living where he lives, from his home built in 1947 by Case Study architect Raphael Soriano, his lush backyard and the views out his windows, from living in close connection to nature, much as he did as a small child.

Although famous for photographing residential architecture, Shulman says it is the nature surrounding the buildings that he appreciates, and it is the balance he establishes between his subjects and their surroundings that make his work so striking and memorable. And make no mistake about it, Shulman remembers it all.

Born in Brooklyn on October 10, 1910—or, as he likes to say, "10-10-10"—Shulman was the fourth of five children. He describes his parents, Max and Yetta, as "literally illiterate about their family backgrounds."

Nevertheless, he recalls from conversations with other family members that his mother on occasion claimed she had arrived in the United States at thirteen—though it was never clear from where (she may have had Hungarian roots). His father's family came from Russia, but given their German surname, Shulman theorizes that his father's families fled Germany to the Baltic states and traveled from there to Ukraine, before immigrating to the States.

Shulman's parents met in Brooklyn and lived, Shulman said, "in a religious Yiddishe neighborhood. They observed all the Jewish holidays." However, opportunities were limited for the Shulmans, and in 1913, Max Shulman decided to move his family to Central Village in eastern Connecticut to become a farmer.

"Why? No one knows," Shulman said.

They lived in what Shulman calls "a decrepit old farmhouse" set on a good piece of land, with no running water, no electricity or heat, save that from a wood stove and kerosene lamps.

Yet the years on the farm in Connecticut were, for Shulman, "a wonderful time of life." His older brother and two older sisters attended the local elementary school. He was the youngest at the time (another brother would be born three years later), and, as a result, stayed at home, free to wander around the farm and spend a great deal of time with his mother, with whom he was very close.

"She was a very understanding, wonderful woman," he said. Shulman attributes many of his interests to his mother.

"We learned a great deal about life from my mother," he said.

Her ability to raise her children in impoverished circumstances, bake bread, milk the cows, skim the cream, run the household, all deeply impressed Shulman.

Wandering around the farm, which was bordered by a forest and had a pond on one end, also had a great influence on Shulman. There were deer, skunks and foxes (much like at his home today, he says). Occasionally, his father would have to rush out to chase a fox away from the chicken coops.

"It gave me a wonderful perspective on life in the natural environment." Shulman said. He recalls his father "on the horse plowing the grounds and planting corn and potatoes, [while] my mother took care of raising the chickens and milking the cows."

However, this paradise was eventually supplanted by another dream. Shulman's father would read aloud to the family from the letters he had received from a friend who had moved from Brooklyn to Los Angeles. The letters said: "Max, you have to come. The streets are paved with gold."

The Shulman family moved first to Norwich, Connecticut, north of New London, where they lived across the street from a synagogue Shulman's father attended regularly. The other families on the street were primarily Polish Catholics, and Shulman recalls the anti-Semitism of the children, who cursed at him in Polish and were, in Shulman's polite words, "antagonistic to us."

For the move to California, Shulman's father went first, found a home and then sent for his family. They traveled by train for five days to cross the country. In Los Angeles, the family moved into a house on Alpine Street, near Sunset Boulevard and Figueroa Street. Shulman's father opened a dry goods store on Temple Street called, New York Dry Goods. In 1920, Los Angeles was a small town with a population of 576,000. Shulman recalls that "living in Los Angeles in those years, no one had cars. We walked to school, my father walked to Temple Street."

At that time, Boyle Heights was becoming the Brooklyn of Los Angeles, that is to say, a thriving neighborhood for Jews. Shulman's father decided to move New York Dry Goods to a new building being built on the appropriately named Brooklyn Avenue (That same street is today called, also appropriately, Cesar E. Chavez Avenue). It was the only dry goods store in the neighborhood and became a success. "We lived a good life."

More important to Shulman was that he was able to find a way to reconnect with nature and the outdoors by joining the Boy Scouts at age twelve.

"It saved my life," he says today.

The troop met at a Methodist church in Boyle Heights on St. Louis Street and camped out on a large plot of land in the Hollywood Hills that had been donated by Arthur Letts, the man who founded the Broadway department store.

In 1923, Shulman's bar mitzvah was at the Breed Street Shul in Boyle Heights. That same year, his father died suddenly at the age of forty-five. Shulman recalls that "my older brother and I went to the shul for yahrtzeit twice a day, early morning and late afternoon, for a year."

"Our background is a very Yiddishe background," Shulman said. "I remember to this day how my mother always observed all the Jewish holidays. Passover is a perfect example. Chametz—clear out all the dishes. We ate a very strict diet to relate to practice," Shulman said (which I took to mean they kept kosher).

His mother and brothers and sisters worked in the store and continued to make it a success (the store prospered even during the Depression). However, he was more interested in being on his own—hiking and camping. In eleventh grade, as a high school elective, Shulman, who had been closed out of an arts course, took a photography workshop, using the family Kodak Brownie. He got an A, but at the time, his ham radio set held more interest.

After graduating high school, Shulman enrolled at UCLA. In 1929, UCLA opened its Westwood campus, and Shulman drove the 15 miles there from Boyle Heights in a Model T Ford he bought for thirty-eight dollars. He started out studying engineering, but after his first year, he didn't re-register and instead just audited classes.

He was in his own words, "just bumming around." As he entered his fourth year of classes at UCLA, his sister gave him a gift of a Kodak "vest pocket" camera. Shulman's first photos were of nature, of hikers, of friends and of his mother.

He recalls taking her picture: "She's sitting by the kitchen window in our house, standing there, working over the sink, and I'm sitting on a chair there nearby." Looking at that same image today, Shulman marveled at the photo—as a work of portraiture. "It's got everything," he said.

When Milton Goldberg, a friend from UCLA, announced that he was moving to Berkeley to get his master's degree, he invited Shulman to join him and audit classes there. This was

Shulman's first experience living apart from his brothers and sisters, "a very private, wonderful life."

With his vest pocket camera, Shulman continued to take occasional photos. They were not snapshots. From the beginning, he used a tripod to stage his images. He entered photo contests, took pictures for a clothing store and sold photos at an on-campus store. But he still had no professional ambition.

When he returned to Los Angeles in 1936, he considered getting a job as a gardener in Griffith Park. His sister was renting a room to a young man who worked for the architect Richard Neutra. Shulman accompanied the young man to a home where Neutra was working and took some photos, which the young man showed the architect.

Neutra, an Austrian Jew with a thick accent, asked to meet Shulman, whom he then asked what he'd been doing professionally. "I told him I'd been in university for seven years. I had been doing nothing. I had no profession." Neutra asked him if he had been studying architecture or photography. Shulman said no, "I was not doing anything; I had no profession." Neutra was surprised. "But your photographs are beautiful," Neutra said. "Would you like to take some more photographs for me?"

As Shulman noted in his book "Vest Pocket photographs": "On Saturday, March 5, 1936, I became a photographer." His career path was set.

"It's a mitzvah," he told me.

On that same day, he was also introduced to another young architect, Rafael Soriano, who was working on his first house. Shulman would photograph the completed home, developing a friendship that would lead Soriano to design Shulman's own home—which he lives in to this day.

As Shulman tells it, his timing couldn't have been better. He was beginning his career in photography just as a number of architects—Neutra, Rudolf Schindler, Gregory Ain, John Lautner, Pierre Koenig and Soriano—were launching their careers.

All this was occurring at the same time that magazines, in particular *Arts & Architecture*, were looking for editorial material, as well as advertisers. Shulman became the go-to guy for photographs of California Modernist architecture.

"I was in the middle of it." Although Shulman did not join his family business, it is clear that he had the family talent for marketing and sales. Shulman explained that he would make several trips a year to New York to meet with editors of magazines, such as *House & Garden* and *House Beautiful,* as well as all the architecture magazines, to gain assignments and make his work known.

"I was concerned with photographing architecture and expressing it, even beyond what the architects themselves saw in their work."

The current exhibition at the Central Library does much to explain Shulman's gift. A section of the show is called, "Staging and Selling the Modern Mystique." In it, we see the final famous image Shulman created, along with other shots that illuminate how Shulman arranged shrubbery or redirected his camera to find the most glamorous angle to best showcase a home. Elsewhere in the exhibition is a shot that Shulman used for a real estate brochure of a completed building, compared to a photo of the actual barren construction site that surrounds it.

Shulman is perhaps most famous for photographing the Case Study houses. The availability of land and variety of terrain Los Angeles has to offer served as a perfect showcase for the work of the Modernists, whose architecture emphasizes the interplay between inside and outside, celebrating the natural beauty of California and taking advantage of the great vistas of an emerging city.

Shulman's success in photographing these buildings came from casting them as outdoor sculptures, functional constructs, whose beauty was realized in organic relation to their setting. Whether his image of Koenig's Case Study House No. 22, a night shot in which the hillside house seems to dangle above the lights of Los Angeles, or Lautner's circular, elevated Chemosphere House, it is the setting that makes the architecture seem both natural and glamorous.

Although the Modernist homes of the time were few in actual number, they served to showcase a particular informal, forward-looking, purely California style of living, and developers sought to adapt the same glamour to their commercial developments. Shulman became the photographer of choice for all such projects.

In discussing Shulman's work, Getty curator Alexander is quick to point out that Shulman was—and is still—a commercial photographer, working for hire. He was employed by the builders of downtown, and when other developers built competing projects, he had no problem working for them.

He was equally at ease taking photos for the Los Angeles Cultural Heritage Commission of buildings worth preserving, as for the developers who sought to (and in many cases did) tear them down.

In the 1980s, Shulman considered retiring from active commissions to focus on book collections of his work, but, as he put it, "I couldn't get away from the requests for my services."

To this day, he is in demand for private and corporate commissions and speaks to students and organizations on frequent occasions.

In connection with the publication of *Modernism Rediscovered*, whose release was timed for Shulman's latest birthday, Taschen is sending the photographer on an around-the-world publication tour.

At one point during our conversation, I asked Shulman about the range of his photography. He told me that during World War II, he was assigned to an Army medical hospital. Shulman said he was "able to make compositions out of the thoracic surgeries."

He also confessed that when he first began to work as a photographer, his friends asked him to take photos of their babies.

"I've got the portraits of babies like you've never seen in your life—beautiful! I was good at it," he said.

He then added, "I was good at anything I did. Still am to this day." He didn't say this in an arrogant way, it was a no-brag, just-facts manner, embued with that touch of amazement that colors every comment he makes about his work, about his life.

Many of the articles I've read about Shulman focus on trying to divine how he comes to compose his photographs—as if it is a mystery that needs solving, rather than a gift.

When we spoke, I asked Shulman if, living in Los Angeles, he was ever interested in shooting moving pictures, in making movies. "No," he said adamantly, not in the least, never. For Shulman, it is all about the composed image.

After our conversation, Shulman took me on a walk around his property. When he was looking for a home in the early 1940s, he remembered the area where the Boy Scout camp he attended had been and drove up Woodrow Wilson Drive to look around. He lives not far from that camp on two acres abutting land donated to a conservancy that will never be developed.

He talked about how his views are unobstructed, how quiet it is, about how the redwood trees that he planted as saplings have now grown to amazing heights, about how he lives in the natural paradise that he loves, that he has enjoyed since his childhood on his parents' farm and continued to appreciate as a Boy Scout camping not far from where he now lives.

Looking around, I confessed to Shulman, "This would make me crazy."

"I'm a city boy; I like to know that people are nearby," I told him. "The sound—and certainly the sight—of animals on my property would make me say, 'It's me or them.'"

Shulman chuckled.

"My brother was the same way," he said.

Shulman told me that his brother lived in a high rise on Wilshire and loved nothing more than going to sleep to the sound of traffic whizzing by on the boulevard below.

This then is the key. Shulman's work, his art, is all about the quiet of the composed picture. His compositions please because they present a sense of calm to the modern world. If you look at his photos, regardless of the subject, you would never call them "noisy," "busy" or "messy." When you ask Shulman about the growth of Los Angeles as a city, he divines no pattern and presents no special insight.

"It just evolved," he answers. "It was organic," he says, much as he describes his career and his life.

Shulman's abiding affection for nature running in parallel with the modernization, industrialization, growth and change of the last century brings to mind another classic—Chaplin's *Modern Times,* in which the Tramp and the street urchin, literally enmeshed in city life, decide at movie's end to leave for the country. Nature, and its balance, have always been the antidote to a modern world that seems out of control.

As the twentieth century evolved, with all its chaos and tragedy, as Los Angeles grew in all its sprawl, as the twenty-first century takes hold with much to fear and much to hope for, Shulman endures in his ninety-seventh year because of his ability to make time stop in his photographs, to appreciate what is before him, to bring an ordered calm to our turbulent times, to take from modernity and make it seem classic. And then, to move on to the next photo—or the next party.

November 15, 2007

DREAMING IN BLUE

Let me state, for the record, that I know nothing about sports. I don't watch them; I don't follow them. My parents didn't. I never did as a kid. I don't now with my family. Occasionally in the finals of a season, a few names flutter into my consciousness and then, just as quickly, disappear. I'm not proud of this. I watch, rather wistfully, as sports informs the conversations of a wide range of folks, as I watch families and friends gather in living rooms or in bars to scream and shout and be together. I have observed all this, yet I am not part of it, and at a fundamental level, I can't understand:

What is the pull of this thing called sports?

It was in this spirit that I approached Roger Director's *I Dream in Blue* (Harper, $24.95), a chronicle of his lifelong obsession with the New York Giants football team and the 2006-2007 season. That I laughed at the many comic moments and was touched by the poignant moments, that I came to understand something of the history and present of the New York Giants, is testament to how good the book is.

Speaking of testaments (what a segue!), Director recounts that the book was prompted by his wife's insistence that he write a will.

"There was a way in which a will was a summarization," Director told me recently over breakfast at Fromin's Deli. "It represented that the best was over, that I was heading back to the clubhouse."

Perhaps a hint of how Director was going to react was apparent when the attorney asked him to name a guardian for his child. Director didn't hesitate for a second:

"Tiki Barber," he said, referring to the Giants' former running back.

Even today, Director still believes he could have eventually convinced Barber, but he could not convince his wife.

So as he was poised to become, in his words, "super-adult," Director decided to reconnect with his "superkid," and spend a season following the New York Giants, a team that has been part of his psyche since the 1956 NFL championship game played in Yankee Stadium, in which the Giants bested the Chicago Bears 47-7 and that he referred to in our conversation as "the native soil" from which all his sports desire grew.

Now would be as good a time as any to reveal that I first met Director many, many moons ago, at a mutual friend's bachelor party. As I recall, Director was trying to talk some of the more inebriated members of the party (it could have been me, but sealed court records prevent me from saying so) off the terrace ledge of a suite at the Morgan Hotel in New York. At that time, Director was a sportswriter, a columnist for the *New York Daily News*.

By the time I turned up in Los Angeles, Director was deep into a successful career as a TV writer-producer on such programs as *Moonlighting* (which gave him material for his 1996 novel, *A Place to Fall*), *Mad About You, Arli$$* and *NCIS*.

In my estimation, Director is one of the more genial people in Hollywood, but as he faced, in his words, "the burden of late middle-aged disappointment," he found himself falling prey to a whole host of issues: He was, on occasion, screaming at TVs and at people in bars (this was Giants related), and he was suffering from restless-leg syndrome, which was keeping his wife up at night. At the same time, his daughter was growing up, and his wife had returned to graduate school. So he decided to revisit his inner child, or in Director's words: "I got all dressed up to date the Giants again."

Sharing Director's "dream in blue" educated me about Giants lore, past and present. I gained an appreciation for the late owner Wellington Mara, coach Bill Parcells and players such as Andy Robustelli and Frank Gifford—names that until now, meant little to me (beyond the Kathie Lee reference). Director has a particular soft spot for Robustelli—a gentleness he ascribes to the player's first name, and the fact that he reminds him in spirit of his father. The scene where Director finally approaches Robustelli at old-timer's day at the Meadowlands is moving and revealing about the mental fortitude that is central to great athletes and so often lacking in mere mortals in general, and overly empathetic writers in particular.

Regarding the 2006-2007 Giants: Director delves into Eli Manning, the quarterback who must suffer the burden of his last name. I also learned that many players are smart, despite what we read in tabloids about their hors concours activities. As Director reiterated to me at breakfast: many are college graduates from good schools, whose attendance of classes one would not want to have to match, and who are compelled for their day job to study, review and retain tremendous amounts of information, even as their bodies receive pounding that few of us could withstand, or even appreciate.

As for Director's man crush on Barber, it continues unabated: "He's a stellar guy. He's an interesting guy because he's a guy with no boundaries in his mind about what he can do. I would not be surprised if Tiki ended up sitting in the Capitol someday."

You heard it here first.

Then there is Tom Coughlin, the Giants' coach, whom Director can't seem to abide. Director rails at Coughlin, whom he sees as a tyrant, unwilling to tailor his approach to best motivate his players. Although he acknowledges that Coughlin "works very hard," Director feels that like getting a great performance out of an actor, "you can't just have one set of rules." But it was more than that. One got the feeling that Coughlin was, in some deep way, an affront to Director's conception of the Giants as a team; an insult, in some way, to the memory of his father—to the gentleness that Robustelli embodied.

I have a running joke with my wife, where she asks what my column is about this week, and I answer: "You know what it's about—it's about me." So, too, Director's book is as much about the Giants as it is about him. Director has made a living writing TV scripts, and given that doing so is generally more lucrative than writing books, or writing for a newspaper, Director will most likely continue to do that for as long as they let him. But I wish that weren't the case.

On some level, *I Dream in Blue* is also about a world in which Director might use writing a book to create a new life for himself. That lets Director return to who he once was, not only as a Giants fan, but as a writer; that allows him to write not about imaginary dramas, but instead about the drama of being himself.

I asked Director whether his restless-leg syndrome had improved since finishing the book. It had not. And I asked whether the child inside him, having had another season in the sun, had been put to rest. Director confided that he had thought that by revisiting with him, he would exorcise him. But the opposite was true; "I haven't been able to get him to go away," Director told me.

That Director's personal saga had no tidy, happy ending made me ponder the difference between our own lives and those we imagine to occur between the covers of a book, or on a sports field, for that matter.

The more I pondered this gap, the more I wondered: Why are sports hailed as "the national pastime"? Why do sports continue to be the most highly rated entertainment programs and such media company profit centers?

I Dream in Blue led me to the following theory: People are passionate, obsessed, by sports because they are events whose outcomes can not be determined—while the games themselves are punctuated by moments of grace, beauty, brute force, elation and victory, as well as boredom, frustration, depression and loss. They linger with the viewers for a moment, and sometimes forever. The statistics, strategies, arguments and conversation arising out of sports are but efforts to know the unknowable. And as such, are endlessly debatable, and for some, endlessly fascinating. But games end, as do seasons.

We admire the athletes not only because they stand in the arena in our places, doing what we can not, not only literally on the playing field, but also metaphorically regarding all those unknowables we seek to avoid. They act as unreflective as we imagine our childhood selves to be (although their reality, like ours, even in our childhoods, are far more complicated).

More importantly, they fascinate because they go on, from defeat as much as from victory, and even after their careers are over and despite their imperfections. They have the capacity to move on, and change even as we are stuck in who we are. That is why we fixate and freeze athletes and sports teams in their moments of greatness. At some fundamental level, they are able to treat what others care so deeply about, as a sport and a game.

We wish and dream (sometimes in blue) that we could do the same.

December 6, 2007

LACMA GETS CONTEMPORARY

In February, the Los Angeles County Museum of Art will unveil the first phase of its renovation and expansion, including the opening of a new building devoted to contemporary art—the Broad Contemporary Art Museum (that's Broad as in Eli and Edythe Broad, our local Medicis) or, as the acronymists at LACMA have dubbed it, BCAM.

On a recent afternoon, I surveyed the new construction with Barbara Pflaumer, LACMA's associate vice president for press relations, as my Virgil. Given the din and scope of unfinished construction, it hardly seemed possible that the work will be completed in time. Yet Pflaumer assured me it will. Mark your calendars: February 16 through 18 will be the opening weekend, free to the public.

However, in order to appreciate why and how these new structures came into existence, it is important to understand the history of LACMA.

In 1910, Los Angeles County inaugurated a Museum of History, Science and Art located in Exposition Park, near USC. The museum's early art holdings were modest but came to include donations from William Randolph Hearst and J. Paul Getty.

In the early 1960s, industrialist Norton Simon spearheaded plans for an independent institution devoted to the visual arts in the Mid-Wilshire district, near Hancock Park, where many of Los Angeles' oldest and wealthiest families lived at that time. Though the idea took hold, eventually Simon withdrew the majority of his own support, opting instead to endow only a small sculpture terrace for the fledgling institution and, instead, eventually morphing the Pasadena Art Museum into the Norton Simon Museum.

Nonetheless, LACMA opened in 1965 with three buildings designed by architect William Pereira, each named after a major donor: Howard Ahmanson, Anna Bing Arnold and Armand Hammer.

Over the next several decades, the museum expanded both its collections and its facilities. On the construction side: A 1983 expansion substantially increased gallery space. In 1986, the Robert Anderson Building for modern and contemporary art was added, and in 1988, the Bruce Goff-designed pavilion for Japanese art (representing the last work by this famed architect) opened, partially funded by Joe and Etsuko Price. In 1994, LACMA purchased the property on the block to its west, including the May Co. building.

On the collections front, there were some major gifts: Joan Palevsky purchased an important collection of Islamic art for the museum; Phillip Berg donated his collection of tribal and ancient art; Hans Cohn contributed his collection of antiquities and glass; and B. Gerald and Iris Cantor presented LACMA with several important Rodin sculptures.

During the same period, the landscape of Los Angeles museums was anything but static. Over the last twenty-five years, a number of new art institutions appeared and have taken root: the Museum of Contemporary Art and its satellites (the Geffen in Little Tokyo, formerly known as the Temporary Contemporary, and MOCA Pacific Design Center); the Hammer Museum (formerly known as the Armand Hammer Museum and now operated by UCLA); the various incarnations of the J. Paul Getty Center (now located in Brentwood and at its original home in Malibu), and the Skirball Cultural Center.

By the 1990s, while these other museums were becoming well established, LACMA sometimes seemed to have lost its focus and its ambition. There was even a three-year period when the museum had no director. LACMA has always been known for having a large and complex board, and as the millennium dawned, efforts were made to rethink the museum's direction.

In 2001, architect Rem Koolhaus (nomen est omen!) was engaged to develop a master plan for the property that involved leveling most of the buildings and constructing a series of pavilions that would take the visitor chronologically through the collection, with different galleries illuminating different cultures' artistic contributions to that historical period.

The estimated cost was $300 million, and because the museum is owned in part by Los Angles County, the funding became the subject of a bond issue ballot initiative that required sixty-six percent of voters' support. When the project received just sixty percent, it was shelved.

Exit Koolhaus. Enter Eli Broad.

Broad, who is a trustee of the museum, was also a huge fan of the architect Renzo Piano, who was one of the designers of Paris' Pompidou Center. As Pflaumer told me, Broad approached Piano, who after seeing the site, decided he, too, needed to develop a master plan, which was named "Transformation" (not to be confused with the similarly named movie by Michael Bay).

The board got involved, and the fundraising began. Broad announced a $60 million lead gift ($50 million as a contribution to paying for a new building and $10 million to an acquisition fund).

According to its own recent press release, LACMA has to-date raised $200 million for Phase I of Transformation. In addition to Broad's gift, LACMA received $25 million from Lynda and Stewart Resnick, $25 million from the BP Foundation, $15 million from Los Angeles County, $5 million from Richard Riordan and Nancy Daly Riordan and $1.6 million from the Ahmanson Foundation.

Piano's plan effectively divides LACMA's campus into three projects or phases. Phase I, which will be unveiled in February, takes the area between the western edge of the original three buildings and the eastern edge of the May Co. (which was primarily occupied by a parking garage and Ogden Street) and re-imagines the space as the new center of the campus.

This manifests itself by changing the orientation of the museum (and I mean that geographically, not sexually), i.e., the new entrance is on Sixth Street, rather than Wilshire Boulevard. Visitors will drive into an underground parking garage and then rise in a glass elevator to a new public plaza, the BP Grand Entrance, an 8,100-square-foot parcel that, according to a LACMA press release, "serves as the museum's main entrance, orientation space and public art plaza." The new plaza will offer arriving visitors their "first experiences with contemporary art."

For the opening, the museum has acquired a major outdoor installation by sculptor Chris Burden, *Urban Light,* made up of more than 200 Los Angeles street lamps that will be powered by the solar panels over the BP grand entrance. In addition, there will also be an installation of palm trees by Robert Irwin, the artist who designed the garden at the Getty Center. From the grand entrance, one takes an escalator that snakes along the outside of BCAM to its top floor (reminiscent of the Pompidou Center, or to inject a local reference, the Beverly Center). BCAM has 60,000 square feet of exhibition space arranged on three floors, in two wings, with a glass core elevator between them the size of a New York studio apartment.

For the inaugural exhibit and for most of the first year, BCAM will focus on artists that the Broads have collected in depth, exhibiting more than 200 works from the Broad Foundation and the Broads' personal collection, including works by such artists as John Baldessari, Jasper Johns, Robert Rauschenberg, Andy Warhol, Cy Twombly, Roy Lichtenstein and Jeff Koons. The ground floor will offer two Richard Serra sculptures, one from LACMA's collection and one loaned by the artist.

As part of Phase I, the Ahmanson building is also being renovated. At the same time, the collection will be reorganized and re-installed not only to showcase highlights from the permanent collection, including some of 130 works by modern masters recently donated by Janice and Henri Lazarof, but also to feature the depth of LACMA's collection in South American, African and Asian art. The former building for modern and contemporary art will become the Art of the Americas building.

Phase II of Piano's transformation will address the May Co. building or LACMA West, as it's now called, as well as building a new free-standing, single-story glass building behind BCAM for temporary exhibitions.

Phase III, which really is in the planning stage and several years off, would address the existing LACMA campus and attempt to reorganize and rethink the displays in those buildings in relation to renovations done in Phases I and II.

Impressive? Yes. But in the spirit of Christmas, (or for my Judeo-centric friends, in the spirit of Charles Dickens) let me say: "Bah, humbug!"

There is something that rubs me the wrong way about this "transformation." The more I thought about it and the order of these "phases," the more it struck me that the logical order was reversed: Shouldn't Phase III, the rethinking of the present campus come first? And why start by building a whole new building devoted to recent art, instead of the current collection and the Lazaroff's newly donated Picassos? Is that modernist collection not as worthy of showcasing as the contemporary works (if not more)? To the extent that LACMA is faulted for being a jumble of buildings, is Phase I a "transformation" or just an addition?

Or, let me put it this way: The fact that Eli and Edythe Broad and the Broad Art Foundation launched the campaign with their $60 million gift, and that Phase I begins with the opening of something called the Broad Museum (not the Broad building or Broad galleries) filled with art that either Broad owns or that he collects (thereby raising the value of his collection or of the artists he collects) bothers me.

Broad has been coy about bequests of his own collection to the museum—he will no doubt, in time, donate many works. However at press time, Broad is merely loaning works to the museum, and no agreement has been reached. Nonetheless, he will also be increasing the value of the works he owns and therefore the value of any tax benefit he would receive, should he gift any of the works.

It begs the question of whether donors and collectors, in general and in specific, and the whole inflated contemporary art market are driving the agenda of the museum, putting an inordinate emphasis on art of the last few decades. Why not leave that to other museums and galleries (MOCA, the Hammer)? Is focusing on the art that the present monied class collects, buys and sells in so extravagant a fashion pandering for their interest and support? Does the fiddler call the tune? Or is it the man who owns the fiddle?

Finally, in so far as Broad's own collection reflects his taste as much as that of his art advisers, isn't this new renovation a collection of other people's ideas used already elsewhere? An escalator up the outside of the building, glass elevators exposed to the outdoors, a Robert Irwin garden, a temporary contemporary exhibit hall—are these distinctive, original ideas? They do nothing to address the present original campus and everything to shmeichel the Broads.

But that is just my being Scrooge.

Several people I spoke to in the art world have high hopes for LACMA's new director, Michael Govan, and for LACMA, believing BCAM and the Broads' support to be essential to revitalizing the institution.

Moreover, when I turned to Lyn Zelevansky, LACMA curator of contemporary art, she cheerily swatted away my objections.

"LACMA," Zelevansky said, is "the people's museum." Located in Mid-Wilshire, she believes it is the museum most Angelenos have access to and grow up with. Also, as a "general museum," it has, Zelevansky said, "a broad audience and our mission is to engage." She believes the BCAM and its emphasis on contemporary art "makes us [LACMA] better."

As Zelevansky sees it, the issue for LACMA was quite simple: "We just really ran out of space."

As for the current frenzy in the art market, Zelevansky said, "The escalation of prices is an ongoing problem."

I'll say. The entire $200 million Phase I transformation would only buy two Picassos, if that. However, Zelevansky feels that while other museums speak to a limited community of art insiders, LACMA, under Govan, is going to use its collections to reach out to Los Angeles' communities.

Pflaumer also told me that Govan intends to engage living artists to create works for the museum that better involve viewers. To that end, the light-filled, columnless galleries of BCAM; the glass elevators; and the outdoor sculptures are all crafted to enhance the visitor's experience of the art.

Alfred Barr, New York's Museum of Modern Art's first director, once said of his own institution: "This museum is a torpedo, its head the ever-advancing present, its tail the ever-receding past..."

With the completion of LACMA's Phase I, it increases its connection to the present and lays the groundwork for its future—one that we hope will celebrate not only the new and the collectible but also the greatness and depth of the museum's encyclopedic holdings. That is a goal worth advancing that even a Scrooge such as myself wouldn't torpedo.

December 27, 2007

KCRW GIVES US 'THE BUSINESS'

In an underground office on the campus of Santa Monica College, Claude Brodesser-Akner is working with his producer, Matt Holzman, and associate producer, Darby Maloney, to describe the current status of the Oscar broadcast—and work in a pun.

Finally, Brodesser-Akner says, with some satisfaction, "The Oscars are mired."

Welcome to the world of *The Business*, a half-hour syndicated radio program devoted to the nuts and bolts of the entertainment industry (pun intended), hosted by Brodesser-Akner each week since June 2004. Produced by KCRW-FM 89.9 in Santa Monica, the show is distributed nationally to public radio stations.

On the show, Brodesser-Akner explores, surveys and comments on all facets of the entertainment business, reaching out to executives, producers and artists, as well as other journalists, that he might not otherwise know, deepening his—and in the process, our—understanding of what is occurring in Hollywood on a weekly basis.

Between drafts of the script for this week's broadcast, which involves a lot of cutting and arguments among Brodesser-Akner and his producers about meaning, nuance, as well as the insertion and deletion of more puns, Brodesser-Akner and I repair to a side office to hear his story.

Long before his 2006 marriage to Taffy Akner, the former West Coast director of education for mediabistro.com, and taking on a hyphenated last name, Brodesser, thirty-five, grew up in Centerport, Long Island, a good Catholic boy. The son of German immigrants, he attended parochial school at St. Phillip Neri in Northport and St. Anthony's High School in Huntington.

At the liberal-arts-oriented Skidmore College, he led a peer-to-peer writing program that taught expository writing, and after graduation, took on a gig teaching English in China as part of a sister school program founded by a former Shakespeare professor.

Returning to New York—by his own account, he "washed ashore, indigent," Brodesser launched into a series of internships that, in hindsight, each "presaged the imminent demise of its editor." Kurt Andersen departed New York Magazine shortly after Brodesser arrived; arts editor Karen Dubin exited *The Village Voice* the week he started; and at the Charlie Rose public television program, the woman he was supposed to report to never appeared, even on his first day.

Nonetheless, in 1996, Brodesser landed his first paying job at Mediaweek magazine, covering TV broadcast stations at what turned out to be an interesting time.

"It was just after the telecom bill was passed," a period that saw a great agglomeration of local stations and outlets.

Brodesser's next stop was at Variety's New York edition, where in keeping with his internship experience, the Broadway editor left shortly after his arrival. Brodesser was given the beat, which he took on, not as a fan of Broadway musicals, but as a reporter—"Just a guy with a pad asking questions." Broadway was a small community, and he sought out *The New York Times'* Frank Rich, who became a mentor and advised him to be fearless.

Variety got aggressive, breaking daily stories.

"It was great fun," Brodesser recalled.

In 1998, as the call of the Internet made a thousand ventures bloom, including sites that hoped to transform entertainment industry reporting (and make its reporters a fortune), such as inside.com and creativeplanet.com, Variety lost most of the members of its film department.

Brodesser moved to Los Angeles to cover film and found it different than New York, where, as he recalled, he could attend a party at Tavern on the Green and walk up to the dean of theater agents, George Lane, and then wander over to playwright Edward Albee—with the understanding that with a drink in one's hand, all comments were off the record.

At Brodesser's first Hollywood premiere in 1999 for the Martin Lawrence-Luke Wilson action-comedy, *Blue Streak,* he approached Drew Barrymore, introduced himself, explained his "drink-in-hand" rule; and they started to chat. He asked her about rumors he had heard concerning the production of *Charlie's Angels.* She answered and then wished him well. Brodesser was delighted to have had a Hollywood moment.

Within minutes, several beefy bodyguards surrounded him.

"Your night is over," they said. "You threatened Miss Barrymore." Despite protestations that he was a member of the press, they picked him up and tossed him out—literally.

Gossip columnist Mitchell Fink wrote about it, and the incident got some play. The next day, Peter Bart, editor of Variety, called Brodesser into his office.

Brodesser feared that Bart was going to fire him. Instead, Bart was tickled pink (and here Brodesser slipped in a British/patrician accent): "That's how you do it," Brodesser recalled Bart telling him, referring to the ruckus he caused. "… That's the way we should do it."

And that pep talk informed his next seven years at *Variety*.

Still nothing could have prepared Brodesser for the call he received in 2003 from Akner, who was then director of education programs for journalism site, mediabistro.com. She called to ask him to teach a workshop. Little did either of them know this call would lead to love, marriage and the baby carriage—not to mention circumcision, conversion, separate dishes for meat and dairy and a hyphenated last name.

As he recounted to me recently, Brodesser was someone who thought he might never get married or have children, but, as he put it, "I met my wife and it was kapow!"

And so, as reported in a New York Times article about their wedding, former Catholic school boy Brodesser, the son of a "father conscripted at age fourteen into the German army near the end of World War II," and former yeshiva student Akner, the granddaughter of "a survivor of the concentration camp at Dachau" and whose concerned mother, Daniela Shimona, prayed for her daughter at the grave of the late Lubbavitcher Rebbe Schneerson, only to have a change of heart when she saw a video about conversions at the nearby Lubbavitch center, were married in 2006.

Brodesser-Akner told me that the thought of raising a child with Akner inspired him to convert. He studied first at the University of Judaism (now American Jewish University), which he felt did a great job of organizing 5,000 years of history and learning into a syllabus. But, he says, "I wanted more." He wanted a conversion that would be accepted by the Orthodox, and his journey led him to Rabbi Yosef Kanefsky of B'nai David-Judea, who became his sponsoring rabbi, performed the marriage and to whose Modern Orthodox congregation the family now belongs.

He says his wife jokes that "her punishment for dating a Catholic boy is living an Orthodox life." They are Sabbath observant, keep kosher and Brodesser-Akner now sports a multicolored kippah.

He says that although being observant is not always easy, "it is worth it." As someone who used to work all the time, Brodesser-Akner is grateful for the respite of Sabbath. But it is the feeling of community—of belonging and caring—that he has experienced as part of B'nai David-Judea that seems to have most deeply impressed him.

Brodesser-Akner explained that although he has lived in a great variety of neighborhoods in Los Angeles and was a very social person, it was only as part of his temple that he experienced a deeper level of community, where each member is cared for. Brodesser-Akner spoke movingly about the visitation schedule organized for a sick elderly congregant and about the attention and care he and his wife received recently in the weeks after their first child was born.

In this last year, Brodesser-Akner also joined Advertising Age as Los Angeles bureau chief, reporting on the entertainment industry (he left *Variety* in 2005 and worked for Fishbow-LA, a mediabistro blog, and wrote for *Los Angeles Magazine,* before being poached for the launch of TMZ.com in 2006, where he lasted a year).

He finds himself at Ad Age at a moment when the industry is in turmoil and the worlds of advertising and entertainment are increasingly converging. To what end, it is hard to say—but that gives him plenty to report and comment upon.

For example, Brodesser-Akner views the Writers Guild strike as "disastrous," not because the writers' cause is without merit, but rather because they are so overmatched by the conglomerates that own the studios and networks that he "doesn't see this ending well." He notes the folly of an industry that claims it can't afford to pay writers, while remaining hostage to star salaries and profit participations.

As for the Oscars, Brodesser-Akner reminded me that last year, fewer than eleven percent of the audience had seen the nominated films. Evidence, he feels, of the disconnect between mega-audience movies and films winning honors.

On the taping of "The Business" that I watched being produced, which aired January 14, the discussion focused on a growing trend to loosen copyright protection on music, as well as an acknowledgement that independent films, such as *The Kite Runner,* might suffer at the box office without award shows, such as *The Golden Globes,* for promotion and publicity.

At the start of our conversation, Brodesser-Akner joked that he had converted to Judaism for the heavy food and self-deprecating humor. But let me take a more Jesuitical—I mean talmudic—approach: Perhaps he did it for the questions. Because, the only thing we know for sure about the entertainment business, based on the past, is that whatever occurs, there will be plenty of questions.

So, beyond the strike and the Oscars remain the questions: Where is the culture going? What will we watch, listen to or play? And on what will we see and hear it? How will it be financed? What will pay for it: hedge funds, product placement, advertising sponsors or Internet ads?

If these questions intrigue you, then the answer is simple. Tune in to Brodesser-Akner for *The Business.*

January 17, 2008

THE GENESIS OF EARLY DYLAN

When it comes to Bob Dylan, I think it's fair to say that I'm a fan of long standing—my wife still teases me about the time, shortly after we'd moved to Los Angeles, when in her car, radio on, she was surprised to hear me as a call-in contestant to KSCA's *Lyrically Speaking* correctly identify the author of the verse in question as, "My man, Bob Dylan."

So you might think that I would be excited to see *Bob Dylan's American Journey, 1956-66,* opening at the Skirball on Feb. 8. But I was somewhat skeptical.

I wondered what there was left to say about Dylan's early career, given the Martin Scorsese documentary *No Direction Home: Bob Dylan* (2005), as well as Dylan's own memoir, *Chronicles Vol. 1* (which I highly recommend for the great descriptions of Greenwich Village in the early 1960s and as one of the best descriptions of how the creative spark grew in a young artist). Also, I questioned what sense it makes anymore to use Dylan, who long ago shunned politics, to illuminate the cultural and social changes of the early 1960s. Finally, I even wondered if a museum exhibition is an appropriate place to tell us anything about a songwriter and his times.

Turns out I was wrong on all counts.

First of all, it's fun to see the many actual artifacts on display; there's Woody Guthrie's guitar and Dylan's copy of Guthrie's *Bound for Glory*. There are handwritten lyrics and inscribed books; there's even the tambourine that inspired *Mr. Tambourine Man* (it belongs to Bruce Langhorne, who today can be found leading the Venice Beach Marching Society and selling Brother Bru-Bru's African hot sauce). There are listening booths where you can hear songs from the seven albums Dylan released during this period, including unreleased recordings and rare documentary footage. There's even an installation where you "produce" and play along to a Dylan track from *Blonde on Blonde*. It's cool stuff.

More to the point, it's brilliantly installed (Robert Kirschner, the Skirball's director of exhibitions, told me it was the most complex installation the museum has ever done). You feel like you are walking through time. You can stop and go back; you can immerse yourself in a moment or a song. It is, for lack of a better word, experiential.

I had been concerned, too, that the exhibit would feel more like being in a Hard Rock Cafe than at a museum, but the informational labels, as well as the audio tour, create a sense of narrative, of history-as-it-happened.

Consider that in just a few decades, we have gone from Garbage-ologists harassing Dylan and family, to all of our garbage being sold on eBay. In this light, a museum exhibition forces us to take the shards of our times seriously (or as T. S. Eliot put it, "These fragments I have shored against my ruins"). There is something to be gained from bringing a critical eye and an organizing discipline to the facts of a life and to the artifacts of an era.

Viewing the exhibition forced me to reconsider some of my idees fixes about Dylan.

I had always thought it somewhat ironic that Dylan, who had a such a deep connection to the work of Woody Guthrie that he came to New York with the goal of meeting him, later rejected the attention of his own fans, telling them "don't follow leaders, watch the parkin' meters."

On many a morning's constitutional, I find myself walking by a home Dylan once frequented yet, despite being an aficionado, I can't imagine myself ever ringing the doorbell (although there does always seem to be a whole lot of gardening going on). The point is that Dylan was not just a fan. He had a purpose in meeting Guthrie.

As Dylan himself relates in the audio tour, at first he had no idea whether Guthrie was alive or not, but then Dylan says he discovered that Guthrie "was in a hospital with some kind of ailment. So I thought it would be a nice gesture to go visit him."

Dylan's desire to meet Guthrie was a way of affirming that Guthrie's work, his life, had meaning—and that Dylan's could as well. But, as I feel compelled to point out, visiting the sick is more than a "nice thing"; it is also a fundamental Jewish value, a mitzvah—bikur cholim—so maybe Dylan did take something with him from the Hibbing shul on West Fourth Avenue or the mysterious rabbi who prepared him for his 1954 bar mitzvah. Dylan's "Song to Woody" would be the first song he felt compelled to write and the start of his journey. Self-invented as Dylan was, the exhibition makes clear that he didn't come out of nowhere. To the contrary, he came out of very specific traditions.

The strength and benefit of *Bob Dylan's American Journey,* which proceeds along both personal and cultural tracks, is that it gives context to Dylan's personal choices and to what the show labels Dylan's "topical songs."

It is hard to appreciate at this distant date how young Dylan was when his career began. He arrived in New York not yet twenty, and in the next year he became an established performer in Greenwich Village. However, he was not yet fully made as an artist and was still pursuing his alternative education, listening to the songs of his contemporaries and their takes on musicians who had come before—and he was reading books that were as much guides as fuel for his creative fires. He was accessing a mother lode, a treasure trove of material, assimilating a world of folk and traditional music and making it his own. He had talent and chutzpah to spare, but working in a genre that blended traditional melodies with contemporary issues, he turned to events taking place around him, and sometimes to the newspaper itself, for material. In the sections of the show on Dylan in Greenwich Village, we can see the raw material of his songs.

The lyrics were political, but Dylan himself was not—he was just processing stories into songs. In the final analysis, and with the hindsight of several decades, those early songs—as much as they garnered attention for Dylan—were not truly his own. Even when they were original, they still seemed to come from someone else (and here's the strangest thing I'm going to say in this article: Listening the other night to Dylan's 1963 Newport festival performance of "Who Killed Davey Moore?" I could swear I heard strains of "Chad Gadya").

One of the weaknesses of "topical songs" is their temporal quality—they were, by definition, of the moment. What Dylan wanted to do, what Woody Guthrie had done, was to write songs that were forever.

It is interesting that in collections of Dylan's songs or greatest hits, beginning with his first collection in 1967 and including *The Essential Bob Dylan* (2000) and the just released *Dylan* in either its 18- or 51-song editions, the collections don't include such protest songs as "Only a Pawn in Their Game" or "With God on Our Side" or "North Country Blues" or "The Lonesome Death of Hattie Carroll"—or even "Masters of War," which has gotten some play during the current conflagration. Only "Blowin' in the Wind" and "The Times They are A-Changin'" seem to make the cut (and even "Blowin' in the Wind," which quickly became an anthem of the civil rights movement, today sounds apart from the rest of Dylan's canon).

As Dylan became one of a kind, he found himself part of a tradition of self-invented, self-created artists who have forged their own way. He rejected the notion of being a leader and even the whole notion of leaders. Yet he remains, as this exhibition demonstrates, "the voice of a generation."

When I listen again, as I've recently been doing, to some of Dylan's most popular songs from his early years, such as "It Ain't Me, Babe," "Positively 4th Street," "Ballad of a Thin Man," or "Just Like a Woman," what strikes me is not the visionary quality but the peevishness—the stubbornness. A lot of those songs, including "Like a Rolling Stone," are put-down songs. That also is very much of his time.

As a child of Depression-era middle-class Jewish parents, coming of age in the 1950s, a decade of conformity, Dylan's stance was one of rejection, one of going his own way—and as such he was as much "the voice of his generation" as Arthur Miller, Rod Serling, Lenny Bruce or J. D. Salinger. His "topical songs" ask Eisenhower/Betty Crocker America to wake up to the reality of racism in the South and the potential of nuclear self-immolation. His more personal or abstract songs expose "phonies" among friends, lovers, music critics—and offer an anthemic call to reject the direction parents, society and the establishment would have us undertake. He is an individualist.

In the late 1950s and sixties, a generation was searching for their own truth, not their parents'. Dylan's disdain, evident in so many of those early songs, is all about staying one's own course. It was about saying "No." Dylan said it to his parents' way of life, to his hometown of Hibbing, Minn., to college and Dinkytown, to the folkies and the protest movement and finally, by 1966, to his fans. He wasn't going to work on Maggie's farm no more.

Similarly, the whole controversy surrounding Dylan going electric is also given perspective when witnessed via the installation at the Skirball and through the prism of those times.

Living in the shadow of the atomic bomb, living through the Cuban Missile Crisis and the Civil Rights Movements, were reasons for high seriousness. But what Dylan displayed from his first appearances, much as Woody Guthrie did, was a sense of humor and a sense of fun (that was often absent from the serious-minded folk scene).

Then President Kennedy was assassinated. Time stopped for a moment there. You might think that such a momentous and tragic event would put a pall on the very notion of "fun," but to the contrary, it was a reminder that leaders are temporal, and time is short. After a proper mourning period, the nation found a way to experience joy again—and it came through music: The Beatles arrived in America.

This exhibition does a great job of making clear that, in retrospect, the question should have been: Why shouldn't Dylan go electric? Not only was The Beatles' sound and spirit infectious, but by capturing the American public (and the record charts), they launched a challenge to all American musicians—a sonic space race, if you will. If the Beatles could access the roots of rock and roll—Chuck Berry and Carl Perkins—why couldn't Dylan, who had been playing Gene Vincent and Eddie Cochran songs in high school and knew that for him, factually and musically, Highway 61 led from the Delta to Minnesota. It was his musical heritage to use.

At the same time, all sorts of performers were already going electric with Dylan's music—The Byrds, The Turtles, even Sonny and Cher had their versions—so, why in the world would Dylan let them have hits with his songs and not decide to join in the fun?

All of which led to an incredibly creative output that would have Dylan, in little more than a year's time, release three albums (one of which, *Blonde on Blonde,* was a double album), producing a cornucopia of songs, bold and funny, mystical and cryptic, full of longing and lyricism.

Several of my friends' teenage children are now Dylan fans, so I thought I would ask them why they listen to or care about his music. I interviewed separately Bijou Karman, sixteen, a tenth-grader at Crossroads School in Santa Monica, and Dakota Nadlman, fifteen, a sophomore at Agoura Hills High School, and they said remarkably similar things. Both came across Dylan through their parents' record collections; both love music from the sixties and had started by listening to The Beatles and then found their way to Dylan.

"I like the sound of his voice," Bijou said. "His voice is so unique," Dakota said, elaborating that Dylan has led him on a journey to listen to all of the artist's influences, from Guthrie to blues artists. For Bijou, Dylan makes her "feel like I was in the sixties." They respond because he and his songs remain real and authentic. As for me, there was a time, not so long ago, when I was wondering why it was I was still listening to Dylan—why buy the latest CD, why go see him in concert?

As I said, I'm a fan but not an uncritical one. I quipped in 2001 that I thought *Love and Theft* was the best album of the year—if the year were 1937. An artist follows his own path, but there is a contract with his audience that, periodically, requires renewal. I had no problem with Dylan sinking deeper into the American roots catalogue, but his Hoagy Carmichael-type and Texas Swing stylings were not really to my taste. So I thought that perhaps I had come to a "Most likely you go your way, and I'll go mine" moment. God knows there was enough Dylan music I liked to fill my iPod, and, as Dylan has pointed out himself, there are many, many cover versions to listen to (there are quite a few good ones on the Dylan 30th anniversary celebration album—and there is even an album of reggae covers of Dylan songs I quite enjoy called, "Is it Rolling, Bob?").

Last summer, however, I somewhat reluctantly accompanied friends to see Dylan perform at the Orange County Fair. To my surprise, he spent the evening on electric guitar and piano, standing the whole time (even swaying/dancing at times), driving his way through a set in which his voice got stronger and clearer (well, somewhat clearer) as the evening progressed.

As I watched, a line from "Song to Woody" came to mind: "There are not many men that done the things that you've done." Dylan was up there, playing his songs, some harking back forty years and more.

There are not a lot of artists like him, doing what he is doing. I felt inspired. I decided there and then that if he keeps his faith with himself, I'll keep faith with myself, and I'll keep listening as long as he keeps playing.

Which brings me back to the Skirball.

Bob Dylan's American Journey, 1956-1966 offers much to enjoy whether you are a hardcore Dylanologist, a rock fan more at home staring at walls in the Hard Rock than in a museum, someone who cares not a whit about Dylan but wants to study the 1960s, or you are (as we might put it on seder night), the child too young to have ever heard of Bob Dylan.

The Skirball's Dylan exhibit sets a context and gives narrative to the emergence of a singular talent who, like his generation, like his nation, were party to dramatically changing times, and who wrote and performed songs that are still being played, by Dylan himself as well as many others, and that will continue to be heard and appreciated as unique and true—even as their provenance and genesis become the stuff of museum exhibits and history.

February 7, 2008

BERNSTEIN'S GREAT WALL

Over the course of a year, I collect books I should read and books I want to read, but—should have/would have/could have—many I never get around to reading. Over the last few months, as last year came to a close and this new one began, and as a side benefit of watching less TV during the strike, I decided to tackle a stack of them.

As is often the case, the books I read could be classified as, to borrow a title from Sergio Leone, "the good, the bad and the ugly." Although the great majority were not worth discussing, one stood out.

Every so often, I read a book that is extraordinary, a book that is so good, so well written, so moving, so memorable that you just want to holler out: Read this! Such a book is *The Invisible Wall* by Harry Bernstein (Ballantine, $14).

The Invisible Wall is a memoir of growing up in Stockport, a small factory town in Northern England, not far from Manchester, in the years just before and following the First World War. It is the tale of Harry Bernstein from age four to twelve and of his Orthodox observant family and of life in the poorest section of town, on a narrow street where one side was populated by Jews and the other side by non-Jews—an invisible wall separating them. Although the book is about the extreme poverty, harsh conditions and bigotry under which they lived, it is also a Romeo and Juliet tale of the romance between his older sister and a boy from across the street.

In no way am I discovering an unknown book. *The Invisible Wall* received glowing reviews in a wide variety of publications, and many features have appeared about the author. Bernstein received considerable attention as an author making his "debut" at the age of ninety-six.

In truth, Bernstein had been published before—a few short stories in his twenties. He had tried a novel in his youth, which was not published. He turned to a career writing for trade magazines. In 1950, he wrote a three-part recollection called, *Twelve Years in a Jewish Ghetto,* for a Jewish newspaper (he was paid a reported $100). Despite this, he did not really return to writing about his childhood until recently.

As Bernstein explained to Mokoto Rich in the International Herald Tribune, two events contributed to his writing his memoir. One, his wife died; he found the loneliness overwhelming and to fill the time he began to write. Second, having lived past 90, Bernstein found that his early memories came back to him so strongly that he had to write them down. He had tried as a younger man to render these stories as fiction, but the truth behind them was too great to fictionalize.

"I realized then why I had failed in writing novels," he said, "because I turned away from personal experience and depended on imagination."

Despite the reviews and features, I was unprepared for the way the book draws you in. "Dickensian" is the word that comes to mind for the world Bernstein describes; "Hobbesian" for the brutishness of his father; "heartbreaking," for the events that oc-cur. I found myself hurrying to pick the book up, yet needing to take a breath at each chapter to recover from the sting of events. All this speaks to the artistry and to the truth with which Bern-stein renders his story.

Bernstein has an uncanny ability to make you appreciate the inner lives of his characters, their dreams, their ambitions, their struggles and disappointment—not only on his side of the street but also in the lives of the non-Jewish residents he comes to know. Bernstein plays a part in their lives, wittingly and unwittingly, and every event is deeply felt.

He was the fifth of seven children born to Polish immi-grants who had come to England and were living in a city where the non-Jews worked in the textile mills, and the Jews in the tailoring shops servicing them. Although their religion informs and insulates their lives, we see how World War I and its casualties bring each side together, and also how the Rus-sian Revolution and the promise of socialism affects the ide-alists among them. (There is a marvelous portrait drawn of a newly arrived young rabbi from Russia, who tells a disbeliev-ing listener about how the revolution, made to promote equal-ity, has already turned against the Jews.) It is a world where bigotry reigns on both sides of the street and where hopes, like Icarus, fall when they dare to fly too high. That being said, the strength of Bernstein's book is that it is not critical or judg-mental. It is a book about surviving one's past—yet cherishing the details of that lost world as well.

The Invisible Wall reminds us of all the things we take for granted from the shoes on our feet, to the food on our plate, to our educations, to our choice of spouse and the way we live our lives. Part of me cries out to read this book to my daughter at night, but that may put me back in the should have category.

In my case, certainly, the reviews were the reason I bought Bernstein's book, but, at the same time, the articles about Bernstein himself may well have been the reason that I didn't get around to reading *The Invisible Wall*: I thought I knew what the book was. I forgot: Sometimes a book transcends what you assume it is by being great.

February 21, 2008

ACTORS GANG CELEBRATES

AN ANNIVERSARY

The Actors' Gang, now in residence at the historic Ivy Substation in Culver City, is celebrating its twety-fifth anniversary. The substation, constructed in 1907 by the Los Angeles Pacific Railroad, looks more like a Spanish mission than an electric power facility, strangely appropriate for The Actors' Gang, which is both a theater troupe with a strong sense of mission and a longtime source of power plays and electric performances (and that's as far as I'm willing to stretch this metaphor).

Over the years, The Actors' Gang has mounted more than 100 productions, including interpretations of Moliere, Ibsen, Brecht and Shakespeare (last summer, they did a children's version of *Titus Andronicus* called *Titus the Clownicus* that was performed for free in Culver City's Media Park).

Recently, I spoke with several founding and longtime members of The Actors' Gang, including Tim Robbins, VJ Foster, Michael Schlitt and Cynthia Ettinger as well as current managing director Greg Reiner, about the past, present and future of the company.

As to the history of The Actors' Gang, Robbins said, "It's a long road, filled with great joy, conflicts that have risen up, [people] who have fallen out [and] egos." That being said, Robbins said that the challenge was "to create a safe environment where people can work."

But first, let's turn back the clock to 1979.

"The company started at UCLA," Schlitt recalled in a phone interview. "A lot of guys bonded playing softball," he explained.

There was an intramural softball league team that featured many future members of The Actors' Gang. Schlitt claimed that, at first, their college major, theater arts, was mistaken for their team's name, and they bonded over the humiliation of so unmacho a moniker.

Robbins recalls it differently, insisting that the team's name was "Male Death Cult" and that its flag was a skull and crossed baseball bats (Foster agreed, adding that they won the intramural championship).

Let's start over: Between 1979 and 1981, there was once a bunch of guy guys who were into theater at UCLA, including Robbins, Lee Arenberg, Richard Olivier, Ron Campbell, Brett Hinckley, Foster, Ned Bellamy, R.A. White and Schlitt.

Robbins was a transfer student, who although born in Los Angeles, had grown up in New York and had been performing and directing plays since he was a teenager. He had attended two years at the State University of New York at Plattsburgh, then came to Los Angeles and spent a year gaining residency before entering UCLA with the goal of performing theater.

This was the dawn of the 1980s, and although President Ronald Reagan and Peggy Noonan had declared it "Morning in America," Robbins was filled with the energy and anger of

New Wave Punk Rock, whose soundtrack was supplied by The Clash, X and Black Flag. In UCLA's theater department and on the intramural teams he found like-minded souls.

In New York, Patti Smith had left theater to find rock and roll and reached back to Arthur Rimbaud and the French Symbolists for inspiration. Robbins decided to take Punk and bring it to Los Angeles theater, and for inspiration, he turned to a French work that launched the Theater of the Absurd, Alfred Jarry's 1896 play, *Ubu the King*.

"*Ubu* was wild, funny stuff," Robbins recalled.

As part of the theater program each semester, students staged a production. Robbins' 1981 production of *Ubu*, assisted by Olivier, was so successful that Robbins and the assorted actors pledged to stage it again.

Foster said the production was compelled by Robbins' energy. Schlitt spoke of "the power of Tim's personality" that made people want to "follow him into the breach." Trying to explain it today, some twenty-five years later, Schlitt said: "We were stupid twenty-somethings."

Robbins recalled that they made a deal with the now-razed Pilot Theater to perform *Ubu* as a midnight show on Friday and Saturday nights. The other production would end by 11, Robbins said, and then they would have an hour to get the stage ready for their production, and they would split the gate. The show ran for about six months.

"We got a great crowd; young people, tremendous reviews." Robbins said.

That original production featured Olivier, Arenberg, and Campbell. Campbell is the one who came up with the company's name "The Actors' Gang."

The company continued working production to production for awhile. Ettinger recalled meeting every few weeks to do workshops where they improvised in commedia dell'arte style.

Over the next few years, The Actors' Gang performed productions of *A Midsummer's Night Dream* in 1984, with Robbins as Oberon and Bellamy as Bottom; *Methusalem* in 1985 with Campbell, Arenberg, Helen Hunt and Ebbe Roe Smith, and the 1987 *Violence,* which Robbins directed and cowrote with Adam Simon and whose cast members included John Cusack and Jeremy Piven (Cusack and Robbins had been in the movie, *Tapeheads,* together).

In those early days, their performances could yield surprising encounters. Schlitt recalled that for a while they performed in a coffee house run by Schmitty, a character who bordered on the savant. One night they heard that Laurence Olivier was coming to see a production of his son, Richard, and there was much anticipation over what would happen when Sir Laurence met Schmitty.

When Sir Lawrence arrived, Schmitty went up to him. Schmitty's words to the great actor?" He treated him like someone off the street: "five dollars gets you a cup of coffee and a seat," Schmitty said. Sir Lawrence, somewhat surprised, paid up.

The 1984 Olympics was, in its own way, a watershed event for the troupe. As part of the events surrounding the Olympics, Los Angeles was home to the Olympic Festival of the Arts, which brought the Theatre du Soleil and George Bigot (pronounced Bee-zO) to LA

"The plays were extraordinary, *Richard II* and *Henry V,*" recalled Schlitt. Several of the members of The Actors' Gang, including Robbins, took workshops with Bigot. "We said: 'This is it.'" They had found the technique they were looking for.

"We had all the energy and the passion, but we didn't have the form or the discipline of how to get there," Robbins said.

The techniques they learned from Bigot became known as "The Style." Some of those techniques involve a very in-your-face, very confrontational form of acting that attempts to engage the audience and is not afraid to have direct eye contact with those sitting in the seats. It also involves focusing on the emotional content of a role as one of four basic emotions: happy, sad, angry and afraid.

"It was a critical development," Schlitt said, echoing Robbins' comments that they needed a way to channel their exuberance.

Ettinger, who joined the company early on, said The Style was highly creative, yet afforded them a discipline. "There's freedom within the form," she said.

Robbins also credits Bigot with teaching them never to take the audience for granted—to regard each audience member as if he spent his last ten dollars and walked ten miles to see their performance—and to never forget that the audience is there to be entertained, not lectured.

One of the signatures of The Actors' Gang has been its ability to workshop and develop plays through improvisational and other acting exercises. Doing so has been a great benefit to actors and writers alike—to be able to start from an idea or a character and develop it into a play.

In 1987, Tim Robbins and Simon cowrote *Carnage, a Comedy,* a play about the rise of the religious right—televangelism with apocalyptic consequences—which is currently being reprised through March 29. The original cast included Arenberg, Bellamy, Ettinger, Foster, Lisa Moncure, Kyle Gass and Dean

Robinson. At the time, the religious right, as embodied by Jimmy Swaggart and Jim and Tammy Faye Bakker, appeared to have more entertainment value than political muscle. But *Carnage* was prescient in speaking to the power and delirium that apocalypse promises.

Carnage, directed by Robbins, had its premiere as part of Pipeline/MOCA's 1987 Angel's Flight series. It was so successful, that in 1988, it opened at the Tiffany Theater on Sunset Boulevard and then traveled in 1989 to the Edinburgh International Festival in Scotland and the Public Theatre in New York.

During the time that *Carnage* was performed at the Tiffany, The Actors' Gang decided to perform another play with it, in repertory—*Freaks,* written by Schlitt and White and directed by Schlitt. Every night, the same actors would finish *Carnage,* a very demanding play, and then suit up for *Freaks,* in which each actor was cast very much against type. For example, Arenberg, very much the dramaturge of the group (Schlitt called him "the playwright's best friend"), played a mute, and Foster, a very physical actor, played Zoltan, a Hungarian gypsy with no body below the waist.

Robbins once told Rolling Stone that in marked contrast to the vanity of most Hollywood actors, "in The Actors' Gang, you find people who want to play characters that are grotesque."

Many of the actors I interviewed recalled the run of *Carnage* and *Freaks* in repertory as one of the artistic highlights of The Actors' Gang. "We were creating really good work," Ettinger said. *Freaks* became one of those talked-about remembered productions. "The results were magical," Schlitt said.

So much so, that this year for the twenty-fifth anniversary of The Actors' Gang, when Robbins asked Schlitt if he would like to revive *Freaks,* Schlitt declined, preferring to let the memory of *Freaks,* in his words, "remain in the ether." Instead Schlitt is directing a revival of Mitch Watson's *Klub,* opening April 11, a play described as *A Chorus Line* meets *No Exit.*

The run of *Carnage* is also worth a footnote for another Actors' Gang performer who appeared in one of its productions—I'll let Schlitt tell the story.

"One of the early productions, 'Inside Eddie Bienstock,' had a small part for a young child," Schlitt said. "His mom would bring him to the theater."

A few years later, White was teaching at Crossroads, and there was a kid who, "rather than go home, used to hang out at White's home, reading. He was like a fixture." He would sit there as Schlitt and White worked on *The Big Show.* It turned out that kid was the same one who appeared in "Eddie Bienstock." "He was very quiet." Schlitt said.

"R.A. White said we should cast him in something; he was really talented. They made him an anonymous soldier in *'The Big Show,* then one day, the kid got his chance to do a full-on role.

"Suddenly, this guy is really talented." Schlitt recalled. "He's got some crazy juice. He has a charisma." Turned out that kid was Jack Black.

It was in *The Big Show* that Black met castmate Gass, who taught him to play guitar and with whom Black would eventually form *Tenacious D.* Black went on to appear in the traveling version of *Carnage.*

Schlitt recalled that one New Year's Eve, he asked Black, "What's your goal for next year? What do you really want to do in life?"

Black answered, referencing The Style: "I really want to work on sadness." I guess he's still working on it—and the rest is the history of Black.

In 1992, The Actors' Gang did a full season at the Second Stage in Santa Monica and then settled in on a location at the El Centro Stage in Hollywood, which they renovated for a year before launching there in 1994

Throughout the 1990s, The Actors' Gang continued to mount challenging productions, including reinterpreting such classics as Buchner's *Woyzeck*, Ibsen's *Peer Gynt*, Moliere's *Imaginary Invalid* and Wilde's *Salome*, as well as such innovative original productions as Tracy Young's *Hysteria*, and her *Dreamplay; Bat Boy: The Musical* and Cintra Wilson's *XXX Love Act* to name but a few. Nonetheless, the facts of these productions do not tell of the complicated growing pains the company faced. In the 1990s, although Robbins continued to be involved, he had moved to New York, was raising his kids and pursuing a film acting career that included *The Player, The Shawshank Redemption* and directing such films as *Bob Roberts, Dead Man Walking* and *Cradle Will Rock*.

As Foster explained, once Robbins had resettled to New York, he was no longer the artistic director. The company had its own management/decision making committee. Robbins had provided funds to renovate and occupy the El Centro space, but he left to them the job, as Foster put it, "to pay the bills."

"We went into survival mode," Foster said.

In order to help pay for the space, they turned to outside rentals, renting the space to other companies, such as David Schwimmer's Looking Glass Company and the Circle X company.

Both Foster and Robbins admitted that one of the problems was that artistic people are not always the best people to run things. As a result, the company had no paid professionals undertaking the job of managing the company, maintaining the space and raising the funds necessary to do so, each of which is a full-time job.

Mark Seldis, who was managing director at the time, told the *LA Weekly* that he was torn as he found his time consumed by administration rather than by creative work.

In 2001, Robbins returned to the company as artistic director. Several members left, among them, Seldis, Young and Chris Wells, according to the *LA Weekly*. Speaking today, Robbins said it was "very difficult to get through that transition."

In 2001, Robbins brought back Bigot to direct a production of Chekhov's *The Seagull* and to conduct workshops to re-introduce old and new members of the company to The Style.

Robbins called Bigot's technique "a liberating approach."

"What you get," Robbins said, "is these amazing discoveries from the actors. It roots the performance in the actor's discoveries." The performance is better, he said, because "they own it."

A new generation of actors became part of The Actors' Gang. Robbins also credited "the new blood" with re-energizing the company. Without singling out any one actor, one can point to Angela Berliner, Justin Zwebe, Pierre Adeli, Stephanie Carrie, Chris Schultz and Matt Hoffman as some of the newer members.

It was also around this time that Reiner joined The Actors' Gang as managing director—the company's first paid professional staff member. Reiner saw great potential in the depth of The Actors' Gang's relationships and in the work it had created.

Productions such as *The Guys, The Exonerated, 1984* and *Embedded* have since gone on to national and international tours. Foster talked about the exhilarating experience of performing in Hong Kong and Melbourne in front of crowds that were almost 2,000 strong.

Robbins credited Reiner with helping him realize that The Actors' Gang was an institution. "We got very lucky with Greg," he said.

As The Actors' Gang found itself on stronger financial footing, it has also expanded its outreach in several ways. The theater offers "pay what you can nights" and student matinees and at least one night during each run is presented for the hearing and visually impaired.

There is now a program for middle and high school students in Culver City, a weeklong workshop at UCLA as well as a program that works in the prisons. There are summer workshops for children and weeklong acting day camps for children as young as eight.

"We are creating work that provokes and invites civic dialogue," Reiner told me.

From its inception, political speech has been part of The Actors' Gang creative energy. "Theater should be a reflection and a reaction to what is happening," Robbins told me. And that has been true for the company since its first production of "Ubu."

For Robbins, this has been particularly true, as he had the opportunity to create works not only like "Carnage" but also, most recently, *Embedded,* which Robbins created in only three weeks and staged three months after the invasion of Iraq. "I don't know a better place to do something quick—to respond to a moment," he said.

As he explained, "We get right up on stage and start working." Yet, as Robbins made clear in our interview, he is always thinking "how do we make this funny?"

Robbins believes that he has a responsibility to the audience to make them ask questions but not to berate them or supply answers. "If you want answers," Robbins said, "go to a lecture."

As for this twenty-fifth anniversary season, attending a recent show of *Carnage*, I was struck by the vitality of the performances—the energy, the physicality.

Directed by Beth Milles, the show's portrayal of televangelists with dreams of power is now an accepted reality. At the same time, when the second act turns surreal, *Carnage* takes on an experimental feel—a combination that some audience members may find unsatisfying. Yet in the end, it is the performances that stay with you—and that reaffirm the vitality of The Actors' Gang.

As part of the twenty-fifth anniversary, *Carnage* will be followed by *Klub*, directed by Schlitt. Irwin Shaw's *Bury the Dead*, a World War I drama, is being considered for the summer. In the fall, they are hoping to stage *The Trial of The Catonsville 9*.

At the same time, Ettinger is creating an ensemble-based piece with music about racism in America. And at year's end, they will reprise Berliner's twisted take on Dickens' *A Christmas Carol*. For Robbins, The Actors' Gang twenty-five years later continues to be, in his words, "a unique situation—essentially a place where I can keep challenging myself."

Foster said that being part of the company "has a been a real joy." For actors, as Robbins pointed out, the danger is always down time. Being able to work—having a place where one can perform—is what it's all about.

For audiences, knowing that there is a theater where we can find actors performing classics and new material that reflect pop culture, even as they challenge, is reason to wish The Actors' Gang a happy twenty-fifth anniversary—and many more.

March 13, 2008

AT THE CROSSROADS WITH ELVIS

Elvis is back in the building.

On March 14 at the Cinerama Dome, Elvis Presley will return one more time in a special fortieth anniversary screening of the "Singer Presents Elvis" special from 1968, or "The Comeback Special" as it is more popularly known, as the kickoff event of the Paley Center for Media's twenty-fifth annual PALEYFEST. A panel discussion afterward will feature Priscilla Presley, his widow; as well as Steve Binder, the producer and director of the special—which is the reason I'll be attending the event.

The Elvis Presley special is far from Binder's greatest accomplishment. A complete list of his film, TV and record productions would dwarf this column, but suffice to say that when *Entertainment Weekly* listed "The Top 100 Greatest Moments in Television," six were Binder's work.

So who is Steve Binder (beyond being my friend Dana Sigoloff's dad), and why was "Elvis" so special that forty years later, people still regard it as one of the greatest TV musical performances ever?

Binder is a Los Angeles native who grew up in Carthay Circle. His father ran a gas station downtown. He attended Los Angeles high and served in the Army.

A friend told him that working at a TV studio was a good place to meet women, so he applied for a job in the mailroom at KABC-TV, the local ABC network affiliate. He quickly rose through the ranks until soon he was directing local programming, including *Soupy Sales*. He then directed the Steve Allen-produced *Jazz Scene USA* and the syndicated *Steve Allen Westinghouse Hour* (at one point directing both at the same time).

In 1964, showman Bill Sargent asked Binder to produce and direct the West Coast portion of the NAACP 's *Freedom Spectacular*, with Burt Lancaster, Edward G. Robinson, Gene Kelly, Tony Bennett, Nat King Cole, Bill Cosby (in one of his first filmed appearances) and Benny Carter in a series of sketches, songs and readings that didn't lecture but subtly addressed issues of race in America. The show was an artistic success, but not a financial one (it was shown in closed-circuit theaters) and, as far as I can tell, was never subsequently released on television, cable or DVD.

Sargent's next production involved Binder filming a benefit rock concert for a foundation that awarded music scholarships to talented teenagers. This became the *Teenage Music International Show*, or *The T.A.M.I. Show*, one of the greatest rock and roll performance films of all times. Jack Nitzsche recommended many of the acts and put together the house band, which included Glen Campbell and Leon Russell.

Filmed at the Santa Monica Civic Auditorium, this 1964 who's who of artists included Chuck Berry, Marvin Gaye, Lesley Gore, Jan & Dean, The Beach Boys, Smokey Robinson and the Miracles, The Supremes, the Rolling Stones and James Brown and the Flames.

Over the next few years, Binder directed a variety of programs, including *Hullaboo* (he suggested having go-go girls in
cages like at The Whisky), *The Danny Kaye Show* (a bad experience), a special for Lucille Ball (a good experience, but a flop)
and two episodes of "Gilligan's Island."

Although Binder enjoyed directing the sitcom episodes, he
observed that in sitcoms, the director was not the name people
remembered. Binder had stumbled into television and directing
almost by chance, and he now had to ask himself: What sort of
a career did he want to have?

Binder had a realization: If he wanted to control his destiny, he would need to produce and direct unique programs for
unique talent, or as he put it, "Tailor-made musical specials for
individual stars." That insight led to some of televisions' most
memorable moments and, of course, to Presley.

But before we get to "The King," it is worth mentioning the
special that got Binder the job, a show in many ways more historic and precedent setting: *Petula*.

Petula Clark was a blond, pixie-ish British singer, who had
a No. 1 hit worldwide titled, "Downtown" (it was the first single
record I asked my parents to buy for me). NBC had made a deal
with Plymouth and its advertising agency, Young & Rubicam,
for a special to star Nancy Sinatra. When Sinatra dropped out,
Clark was recruited.

Binder decided to pair her with Harry Belafonte as a guest
star. Some executives at Plymouth objected, but Binder insisted.

Although it was 1968, some advertising and auto executives
were anxious about a white woman and a black man appearing
in a national TV program together. I know it sounds crazy and
hard to believe, but there was a moment in the show, unscript-

ed, when Clark touches Belafonte's arm—"the touch," Binder calls it, that was taken to be of such historic importance to race relations in America that Newsweek sent over a photographer and *The New York Times* and others ran articles about it.

In spite of this (and perhaps because of it), the show was a success. And that led to Binder receiving a call to meet "The Colonel."

TV producer Bob Finkel told Binder that NBC's Tom Sarnoff had struck a deal with Presley's manager, Col. Tom Parker, to do a special, but Presley was reluctant to return to television. Finkel felt Presley and Binder would hit it off, and that, based on Binder's experience on the *Petula* special, Binder would be able to stand up to the Colonel. Binder was not an Elvis Presley fan, but his partner, Bones Howe, a successful music producer, said he would be crazy not to meet him.

After a successful meeting with Finkel, Binder and Howe went to meet the Colonel at his offices on the MGM lot (what is today the Sony lot in Culver City). The Colonel dominated the whole meeting, telling grotesque stories from his carny circus roots and bragging about his deal-making business acumen (Binder said he was repulsed by the former and unconvinced as to the latter).

The first meeting with Presley took place, Binder recalled, on May 10, 1968, at the Binder-Howe offices on Sunset Boulevard (next to the old Tower Records store). Presley arrived on time with his entourage of four friends, who sat in the waiting room as Presley met with Binder, Howe and Alan Blye and Chris Bearde, who would write the special. Presley had not appeared in front of a live audience in years. Binder reassured Presley, telling him that if they worked together, "he could focus on making records, while I would put pictures to his music." Presley signed on.

One day during rehearsals at the Binder-Howe offices, Binder said he saw Presley looking out at Sunset Boulevard—and in what is now a legendary story—Binder asked Presley what he thought would happen if he walked out on Sunset by himself. Presley asked Binder what he thought would happen. Binder thought about it and said: "Nothing." A few days later, Presley turned to him in the office and said, "Let's go."

Much has been made of what happened next: Presley stood with Binder on the street in front of the office building, at first tentative, then surprised that no one recognized him, then somewhat disappointed that no one recognized him and then, finally, uncomfortable. Presley retreated back to the offices.

The special was recorded at NBC's Burbank Studio No. 4. Presley was so impressed with the dressing room suites that he decided to live at the studio during the recording, asking that an upright piano be brought into his suite.

Binder noticed that Presley and his musicians would hang out in the suite's living room, before and after rehearsals, joking around, playing songs, talking about old times. Binder realized that this is where Presley was most comfortable, and that the public had never seen this side of him.

Binder decided that he wanted to film these "jam sessions," and after a consultation with the Colonel, they decided to recreate that feeling by having Presley and his original band members (who at first were not part of the special) seated in a circle on chairs on a small stage, surrounded by an audience. The special itself used these performances sparingly but to great effect. (Over the years, those "improvisations" have taken on a life of their own, as reassembled into a separate special aired by HBO, *One Night With Elvis*.)

Watching the special recently in my office, I was struck by how good it still is. Presley's vitality, his sense of humor, his charisma, his sex appeal and his connection to his music and his love of performing come through in an indelible fashion (only some of the dance numbers seem dated). No one who sees the *Elvis* special can doubt his appeal or his talent.

Elvis aired on Dec. 3, 1968, and captured forty-two percent of the entire viewing audience. It was NBC's biggest ratings victory for the entire year and the season's No. 1-rated show. However, after the show aired, Binder never really spoke to Presley again (he believes that was the Colonel's doing).

For the *Elvis* special Binder was paid a contractual one-time payment of $32,000 for producing and directing, which included the first two reruns of the special, and a $3,500 payment for each of the third and fourth reruns. That was it. No DVD or ancillary rights (they didn't exist). And certainly no "artistic rights of control": every re-edit or rerelease of the *Elvis* show since, in regular and deluxe editions, including the HBO special, and whatever will be screened at the Cinerama Dome, were done without consulting Binder (or paying him a penny more).

Nonetheless, Binder recalls *Elvis* fondly.

Binder believes that during the making of the special, Presley reconnected to making music he believed in. Presley told Binder he had found his "freedom"—the ability to be himself again. But that freedom was short-lived.

After the special, a galvanized Presley recorded such hits as *Suspicious Minds, In the Ghetto* and *Kentucky Rain*. He also appeared for several record-breaking performances in

Las Vegas before embarking on a national tour. Binder saw Presley perform then, saying "he was fantastic."

However, a year later, he saw Presley perform again and found that he had lost his spark and was bored. (Neither time did he go backstage to see Presley.).

"I knew then," Binder said, "that it was over."

In his last Vegas performances, an overweight Presley became a parody of himself, a Liberace-like performer who turned his back to his audience and increasingly found it hard to finish a show, or a song for that matter.

On August 16, 1977, Presley was found dead in his Memphis home, Graceland, the victim of a heart attack, his health having been compromised by drug abuse. He was forty-two.

For Binder, the *Elvis* special was but one landmark in a career that continued to expand and unfold. Binder went on to direct many, many, many more specials for a wide variety of stars, including (to name but a very few) Barry Manilow, Diana Ross (including the memorable *Diana Ross in Central Park*), Patti Labelle, *Divas 2000* for VH-1 (featuring Ross, Donna Summer, Mariah Carey, Faith Hill and Beyonce); events such as the half-time show at the 1996 Super Bowl, *The Star Wars Holiday Special* (a sought-after bootleg—by geeks that is); films such as *Give 'Em Hell, Harry* (for which James Whitmore was nominated for best actor), and was involved in the careers of many recoding artists, among them Seals & Croft. He is currently managing the career of Italian singing star Nicola Congiu.

Binder, for one, certainly never imagined that forty years later, audiences would still be gathering to watch the *Elvis* special.

But people keep coming back to the special. I think I know why: *The Comeback Special* presents Presley at a juncture—his past, his potential, his talent—and the intimation of the tragic path he would unfortunately choose. It's all up there on the screen: The softness in his face that made him look boyish, the full lips that look almost feminine (and that would appear so strongly in the face of his daughter, Lisa Marie). There he was in black leather, with his animal grace and his magnetism—his sex appeal as much at his command as his laugh. His self-deprecating humor and the easy familiarity with which he kidded around.

You see the way he responds to the audience and the audience responds to him. You see Presley in full command of his talent and power, "The King," with the potential to remain one of the greatest rock and roll entertainers of all time.

At the same time, the show contains all the foreshadowing of what was to come. The face that would bloat, the distracted manner of starting a song and not finishing it, stopping to break into a joke, not taking his talent or his songs seriously, changing the lyrics as a goof, wiping the sweat off his brow with a handkerchief for a woman in the audience, the large production numbers, the faked emotion, all the signs of his impending tragedy are present.

That's why the show has remained memorable, because we catch Presley at the crossroads. He has emerged on Sunset Boulevard, and he has a choice: to embrace his music and his audience or to retreat into the Elvis Presley cocoon.

Binder's career has been one of granting the audience memorable performances by singular talents. However, in *Elvis*, he caught a legendary artist at the intersection of his talent and his destiny, at a crossroads to which he would never return.

Elvis chose to go back in the building.

March 13, 2008

WHERE WILL THE

BOOK-LOVERS GO?

D utton's Brentwood Books, among the best-known and
best-loved of Los Angeles' independent bookstores,
will close on April 30.

It is hard not to take this as a sign of the times.

Over the past few years many local independent bookstores
have gone the way of the local movie theater, the local hardware
store and the local stationery shop—disappearing—as much
victims of a changed retail and commercial real estate environment as a victim of our changing consumer and lifestyle habits
(more on that later).

All my favorite haunts of my post-grad years in New York
have vanished: Books & Co., the Madison Bookstore, Canter-
bury Books, Shakespeare & Co. In Beverly Hills, no general
bookstore remains, only Taschen's retail outlet. In Santa Monica, we have lost bookstores big (Crown) and small (The Book
Nook in the country mart).

However, to paraphrase Shakespeare, that best-selling author, we have come not to bury Dutton's but to recall the good
times.

First some history: Doug Dutton's parents were booksellers and ran Dutton's in North Hollywood, which Doug's brother, Davis Dutton, took over after them (and then closed in early 2006). Doug Dutton opened the Brentwood location in 1984.

Dutton's extends across several different rooms on the ground floor of a two-story building on San Vicente Boulevard, and at its heart is a central courtyard that seems tailor-made for readings and book parties. The site also provides ample parking behind the building (an important draw in Los Angeles).

The two-story U-shaped building, with its stairways lining the central courtyard, have always reminded me of those Bauhaus-style structures that dot Tel Aviv and are meant to express a functionality in harmony with the Mediterranean climate and an indoor/outdoor lifestyle. How toddlers love those stairs! How parents eyed them nervously!

Dutton's itself occupies almost 5,000 square feet. The main room, on the west side of the building, is filled with literature, mysteries and current non-fiction in both hardcover and paperback. To the north is housed the non-fiction, as well as music offerings and audio books; to the east are the children's room, the travel books and cookbooks, and the gift and stationery items and, a relatively recent addition, a cafe.

The whole place always had a ramshackle feel, with frayed carpets and crowded shelves. Each area is its own empire, and one felt free to wander among them, and trusted to take a book from one area to the other without being accused of running off. The staff has always been friendly, knowledgeable and, on occasion, eccentric (Dutton's had a staff poet in Scott Wannberg).

Oh the book signings and parties I've attended at Dutton's! Lots of white wine and cheese cubes under the bridge. Dutton's was a place where you went to support your friends, to buy copies of their books, to hear them read. I recall attending events for friends such as (alphabetically) Robert Cohen, Roger Director, Seth Greenland, Mona Simpson and Deanne Stillman (and those are just ones I remember). Dutton's was a place you took your out-of-town friends to show them what Los Angeles had to offer in book culture. It was where you took your author friends to ask Dutton to let them sign copies of their books. It was a place you went to get a peek at your writing idols when they came to town.

I myself had one or two book events at Dutton's, and the feeling of sitting behind the counter and looking out at a room of friends and readers crowded between the display tables was a heart-warming sight for any author. It made a writer feel, for a long moment, part of a community.

Dutton's was old school: I had a house account there that allowed me to sign for books for which I was billed monthly; my ten-year-old daughter had signing privileges on my account. I had imagined the day would come when she would have her own account, but that is not to be. (This reminds of the time my father was approached about buying a "lifetime membership to a health club," and he replied, "My lifetime, or your company's?" He outlived that business by several decades.) So it goes.

No more stopping by on a Saturday afternoon to wander among the display tables, to run into friends, to discuss new books, to recommend favorites. No more going to get a signed first edition of a friend's new work (talk about an author's heartbreak: Mark Sarvas was scheduled to read from his new novel, *Harry, Revised,* at Dutton's in early May; Dutton's closing on April 30 forecloses that, as well).

Which brings me to Dutton's closing—who to blame and what to do about it?

One could blame a world in which handbags regularly sell for more than $1,000, where coffee can cost more than four dollars per cup and a tart frozen yogurt is a five dollar treat as explaining a retail environment that demands a greater return than books can deliver. Or an inflated real-estate market that calls on developers to achieve a greater return than the current structure can deliver—but Doug Dutton himself will tell you that the developer who owns the building, Charles Munger, who plans to redevelop the property into something more high-rent, is not the villain here. From Dutton's announcement of his store's closing:

"Given our situation as it now stands, the pride we feel in our past achievements, and the vagaries of the current book market, shuttering our doors seems the only realistic solution. It is important to note that Charles Munger has committed to a significant amount of financial support for the difficult process of closing the store, and we appreciate his generosity."

In 2004, Dutton's opened a Beverly Hills branch with incentives from that city, but when those conditions changed, the bookstore could not continue and closed at the end of 2006. More than anything, it was the difficulty of being a bookseller in the current marketplace. I remember a conversation with the owner of the Book Nook before it closed. He told me that people's habits have changed. Today, the majority of bestsellers are purchased for forty percent off at Wal-Mart or Costco. The small book that becomes a success because of independent bookstores has become as rare as the independent movie that succeeds by word-of-mouth—it happens, just not often enough to sustain a business.

There continue to be, and there will be continue to be, great independent bookstores in Los Angeles, from Skylight Books in Los Feliz and Book Soup in West Hollywood to Village Books in the Palisades and Equator Books in Venice.

However, this is the way we live now: If you want to see a busy bookstore, go to an airport. The enemy, as Pogo said, is us. I need only look to my own buying habits. If there's a book that I know I want, either a new title or an obscure one, I will often buy it from Amazon.com or AbeBooks.com. I spend a certain amount of time browsing at Borders or Barnes & Noble, but I can't tell you the last time that I bought a book there because of a bookseller's recommendation (at press time, Border's has put itself up for sale). Times change, customs and behavior changes and Dutton's is just one sign.

I stopped by Dutton's this week, and while I won't go as far as to call it a shiva visit, as I crossed the courtyard I spied two successful TV writers bemoaning Dutton's closing. Seeing Doug Dutton, one woman got teary, talking about how she had grown up with Dutton's and what the loss of the bookstore and its community means to her.

Which brings me to another point. Dutton's, like any good independent bookstore, represented more than a retail enterprise, and its closing affects our quality of life. The question then becomes one of whether we could change the market reality of bookstores. Can we instead protect, encourage, support and value those aspects of places like Dutton's that mean so much to us?

Where will we go to get that sense of community, that feeling of being in a place where books are a valued part of our culture? Where can I take my daughter to imbue her with that same sense?

In a world where the bookstore is less and less viable, where do we go to find like-minded others of all ages who enjoy books and other cultural delivery systems such as graphic novels, comic books, games, videos and CDs? Where can we go to see and hold in our hands not only current titles but also a long tail of widely diverse offerings—where will we find knowledgeable guides to help us find what we are looking for or make suggestions? Where can we go to see our literary idols?

Perhaps Dutton's closing is a sign of our times. I will miss it, and we—our community, our city, our world—are the poorer for its loss. Perhaps the bookstore is no longer commercially viable. But we need not abandon the bookstore experience.

Again, I can only turn to my own experience. I will tell you where I go: To the public library.

Recently I stood at a display case in the Beverly Hills Public Library reading original copies of letters written by Dashiell Hammett, James M. Cain and F. Scott Fitzgerald. Last week, I was at the Central Library to hear Richard Price talk about his new novel *Lush Life*.

Perhaps when Dutton's closes we need not feel we've lost all we value.

Have you visited the Santa Monica Public Library's new main branch? Not only is it airy and comfortable with plenty of parking, not only is there a great kids area that has books and computers with games, but for those who got used to associating a bookstore with noshing, it also houses a great and reasonably priced cafe.

Stephen Schwartzman of Blackstone Group recently announced a $100 million gift to the New York Public library—a rare but inspired gift. More often the case these days is the library that is laying off staff and is hard-up to buy new books. Those that thrive do so with community support. It will take more donations and public support to libraries and "friends of the library" groups to keep our cultural communities strong. However, if the marketplace can't support bookstores, and we still believe that books bring people together, we will all have to do our part to affirm the value in people coming together in a place that values books.

April 3, 2008

SET A PLACE FOR SHATNER

AT THE SEDER TABLE

William Shatner is God. And Pharaoh. And Moses, too. Just in time for Passover, the Jewish Music Group (a division of Shout Factory) has released *Exodus: An Oratorio in Three Parts*, performed by the Arkansas Symphony Orchestra. It is conducted by David Itkin, who created and composed the Oratorio, sung by baritone Paul Rowe and includes dramatic readings from the Bible and from the haggadah, spoken by none other than Shatner.

"It's perfect seder entertainment," Shatner said recently, but more than that, "it speaks to people of all religions. It's something that should be in repertory."

Exodus: An Oratorio is divided into three parts: "Moses and Pharaoh," "The Ten Plagues" and "Redemption." The music mixes symphonic and sacred, modulating strings, choral voices and baritone solos to provide both uplift and ballast to the biblical material—as well as gentle musical transitions between some of Shatner's narrative performances. While Shatner has been parodied for his ability to bring a level of bombast to almost any material, here he gives a varied and nuanced performance—his voice varies from sounding like a pulpit rabbi to the muted and conversational tones of a line reading. And then there are the special effects that are his signature—when he makes his words pop with emphasis: (i.e., I...AM...THE...LORD!)

Exodus was recorded live on April 9 and 10, 2005, at the Robinson Center Music Hall in Little Rock, Ark., where the Arkansas Symphony was joined by a choir of 350.

"It was quite a happening," Shatner recalled in a recent telephone interview.

The work is just one of a number of new projects for the actor, who turned seventy-six on March 22. In the next few weeks, his autobiography, *Up Till Now,* will be released, as well as a DVD of *William Shatner's Gonzo Ballet,* which is a feature-length documentary about a ballet based on Shatner songs from his Ben Folds-produced album *Has Been.* And, on April 26, he will host his annual event, Hollywood Charity Horse Show to raise money for a therapeutic equestrian program for handicapped kids.

To listen to Shatner tell the story of Moses, Aaron and Pharaoh, to hear him read of the ten plagues and the story of the parting of the Red Sea, mixed in with choral and solo performances in English and Hebrew, is to realize how much of an icon he has become and what an amazingly diverse career he has had.

Shatner was born in Montreal, Canada, to Jewish parents and grew up in a kosher home. As a teenager, he was a counselor at a B'nai Brith camp in the Laurentian mountains in southern Quebec, according to various Web sites. He attended McGill University, earning a bachelor's degree in commerce. However, by the time he was twenty he had already landed a small role in a Canadian TV series. Over the next decade, Shatner would perform Shakespeare and appear on the Broadway stage in Christopher Marlowe's *Tamburlaine The Great,* as well as the Richard Mason play *The World of Suzie Wong,* and the Harold Clurman-directed *A Shot in the Dark,* alongside Julie Harris and Walter Matthau.

During the 1950s, Shatner appeared in several of the "golden age of television" dramas, such as *Omnibus, Studio One* and *The Kraft Television Hour,* including *A Town Has Turned to Dust* directed by John Frankenheimer and written by Rod Sterling. Shatner also had roles in such now-classic films as *The Brothers Karamazov* (with Yul Brynner and Claire Bloom) and "Judgment at Nuremberg."

A list of Shatner's credits from the early sixties includes almost every famous series, including *The Twilight Zone, 77 Sunset Strip, Route 66, The Outer Limits, The Defenders, Dr. Kildare,* and *Gunsmoke.*

In 1966, he assumed command of the Starship Enterprise, as Captain James T. Kirk. Although only seventy-nine original episodes ran between 1966 and 1969, the *Star Trek* series cemented Shatner in the popular consciousness.

Nonetheless, after the series was cancelled, and following a divorce, Shatner was forced to live out of his truck, performing summer stock. During this period, concerned that he had been typecast as Kirk, Shatner wandered in the wilderness, taking whatever roles he could.

He returned to the helm of the Enterprise for the six Star Trek movies (directing the fifth). And he also returned to TV as the star of the police drama *T. J. Hooker,* and then to host the reality series *Rescue 911.*

At the same time, Shatner began to display a sense of humor about his long tenure as Captain Kirk, and the legions of obsessed Trekkie fans, in such films as *Airplane II* and *National Lampoon's Loaded Weapon* and in skits on *Saturday Night Live.* He gained further notoriety as a pitchman for Priceline.com.

More recently, Shatner hit gold again, portraying attorney Denny Crane on *Boston Legal,* a role he originated on the series *The Practice.* He is one of the few actors to receive consecutive Emmy awards for playing the same character on two different series.

Shatner's life has also had its share of tragedy: his third wife, Nerine, drowned after mixing valium and alcohol. Shatner recently told Details magazine that he didn't "understand closure …we grieve forever."

As for his recording career, it began with his much-derided 1968 album, *Transformed Man* and with his over-the-top spoken word interpretations of songs such as Bob Dylan's *Mr. Tambourine Man.* In 2004, Ben Folds produced *Has Been,* a collection of songs, many of which he co-wrote with Shatner, including featured guest performances by Joe Jackson and Aimee Mann. It was well received and became a commercial success.

Which brings us back to "Exodus" and its composer David Itkin.

Itkin grew up in a conservative Jewish home, began writing music at fourteen and conducting at sixteen. A graduate of the University of The Pacific Conservatory, he has been music director of the Arkansas Symphony since 1993, while also conducting and serving as music director for the Abilene Philharmonic Orchestra. It has just been announced that he will leave The Arkansas Symphony after the 2008-2009 season to become director of orchestral studies at the University of North Texas at Denton. At a seder in 2003, Itkin said he was stuck by the dramatic possibilities of the Passover story. He developed the composition while on sabbatical in Florence, Italy, the following summer and fall.

When Itkin secured a 2005 date for the *Exodus Oratorio* he still needed a narrator. "We kicked around lots of names," he said, and always considered but was not wedded to using famous Jewish actors. "We kept winnowing and winnowing the list" he said, "and Shatner's name kept coming up. And it wouldn't go away."

Itkin contacted Shatner, and it turned out that not only was he interested, he was available on the needed dates.

"It was intriguing," Shatner recalled.

So with little preparation, other than years of reading the haggadah at seders, Shatner arrived in Little Rock the night before the first performance.

"He was great fun to be around," Itkin recalled.

There were two rehearsals and two performances—one on Friday and one on Saturday night. Itkin was impressed by how Shatner was able to deliver his narrative within the very proscribed places and vary each character, much like different "takes," affording choices for editing the eventual produced work.

"On Saturday," Shatner said, "everything fell into place." He reveled in the experience of being on stage with 350 choral members and a seventy-two piece orchestra, he said.

"There's no magic like a live audience," Shatner says in the recording's liner notes. "The performer sends out the words, the music, the love, and he gets back the energy of the audience in waves."

In the final section, "Redemption," he intones the words of the priestly blessing: "May the Lord Bless you and keep you; may he be gracious to you; may the Lord make the light of his countenance to shine upon you; and may he grant you peace."

"The words were like a benediction over the whole audience." Shatner recalled.

At the seders I attend, I am not above some moments of audio-visual enhancement. I recall one spectacular seder where, at the strategic moment, the late Charlton Heston burst onto a screen to part the Red Sea. In recent years, the immediate post-seder entertainment has been funny Passovers songs (like "There's No Seder Like Our Seder" to tune of "There's No Business Like Show Business"). This year may well find our seder going forth with Shatner and the *Exodus Oratorio*.

And let us all together say: Amen.

April 17, 2008

POST-ZIONISM IN A

DIASPORA WORLD

What does it mean to be a Jew in a Post-Zionist world?

For centuries, for Jews, the notion of living free in Zion was a dream. In Theodor Herzl's famous essay, "The Jewish State," the journalist and playwright transformed the dream of living in a Jewish state into a goal.

"Next year in Jerusalem," the words we say at the end of every seder, was in those days a true aspiration for nationhood. Today, it is often treated as the lead-in to a joke whose punch line is, "And if we're lucky, next year at…(fill in the blank for someone's home or any luxurious destination)."

The notion that all Jews should one day live in Israel was very much part of my own childhood Hebrew school education, and I recall many elders talking about their dreams of retiring to Israel or being buried in Israel.

As I was growing up, it seemed that Jewish immigration to Israel, making aliyah, was the silver lining to be found in every contemporary Jewish Diaspora calamity: Soviet Jewry is suffering? Then let them go...to Israel. Ethiopian Jews in trouble? Airlift them...to Israel. More recently, after calamities in Argentina and anti-Semitic attacks in France, incentives were offered to families to move to Israel. Yet I imagine these campaigns were less successful than those of my youth. In part this has to do with the global community we live in now.

Here in Diaspora Los Angeles 2008, Israeli culture is woven into my daily fabric: On any given day, I can find myself watching an Apple Computer commercial featuring "New Soul" by French-born Israeli singer Yael Naim, or watching HBO's *In Treatment,* which is based on an Israeli show. A recent *LA Weekly* issue carried a profile of short story writer and filmmaker Etgar Keret written by film critic Ella Taylor, who once lived in Israel herself.

Israelis seem to be everywhere—at the mall, all the kiosks are manned by Israelis; the most popular vendor in the food court sells shwarma; and Krav Maga, an Israeli martial art, is taught just down the street. Santa Monica might be home to more British citizens, but I just seem to notice the Israelis.

Once upon a time, Israelis living here would have been viewed as disloyal—dropouts. Today, they are just another ethnic community placing a stake in Los Angeles.

This is post-Zionism.

As Israel celebrates its sixtieth anniversary, it seems that we have entered an age where living in Israel is no longer the goal of all, or even most, Jews in the Diaspora—even for some born there. This begs the question, what then is Israel in the hearts and minds of today's Jews? What should it be?

Israel was founded as something of an agrarian socialist utopian society—its form of government inspired by the Mensheviks. The kibbutz was the soul of the country. But that hasn't been the case for several decades. What is the soul of the country today? Its high-tech industry? Its army?

Perhaps it is Israel's diversity.

In a recent interview in Germany's weekly Die Welt, author Amos Oz said, "When I look at the German or other European media and see that image of Israel it creates, I learn that Israel supposedly consists of eighty percent religious fanatics, ten percent settlers in West Jordan, nine percent brutal soldiers and 1 percent intellectuals who criticize the government and who are wonderful writers. This is of course a distortion of reality."

The reality is that Israel is a country that prides itself on having at least one of everything (from ski mountain to Dead Sea, from tofu factory to star fruit farm); what doesn't Israel produce, manufacture and what can't you do there? Israel has produced world-class literature and has a vigorous free press that voices every opinion on every side of every issue and uncovers every scandal, and it has a Supreme Court that has come to be the moral conscience of the country.

Nonetheless, one can argue that the main impact of post-Zionism has been to make Israel less self-absorbed and the Diaspora more so.

In Israel itself, sixty years of existential peril have created a sense of living in the moment—currently there is a surprising sense of well-being among certain strata of the Israeli population that comes from focusing on family, on work and on materialistic concerns divorced from national and political concerns. When you live in the moment, you can live anywhere: This, in part, explains the lessened stigma of being an Israeli who chooses not to live in Israel.

By contrast, for Jews in the Diaspora, while Israel remains a touchstone in their hearts and minds, and the life-changing trip to Israel is a de rigueur experience, there is nevertheless a growing malaise about Israel and its policies, whether you are on the far left, or the far right. This is true even among people like me, who consider themselves centrists, but who are too left for the right and too right for the left.

I am reminded of the Israelites in Exodus who, when delivered from Egypt, began to complain, and continued to complain at each turn—about being in the wilderness, about the food, about their thirst and on and on. In a similar vein, it strikes me that the age of post-Zionism is also the age of complaining. There may even be a reason for it.

In the mid-1980s, Israeli archives adopted a liberal policy of declassifying official documents, giving historians and journalists access to troves of official papers related to Israel's founding and early years. Many historians, most notably Tom Segev and Benny Morris, began to search out the truth of those early years. In time, they and others, collectively referred to as "the New Historians," wrote a series of books about the mandate era, the war for independence, and the 1967 Six-Day War—revisiting the pillars of Israel's national story—the most recent of which is Morris' just-published *1948—A History of the First Arab-Israeli War* (Yale University Press). As these accounts have been translated into English, journalists, historians and readers alike have had to confront some difficult facts.

Contrary to the national narrative of manifest destiny that Jews in Israel and the Diaspora had come to accept as gospel, the history of Israel turns out to be far more complex. The historical record reveals what had been hidden or glossed over in the service of nationalism: That in birthing a nation, the Israelis did not all have clean hands—Arabs were expelled, their villages destroyed, massacres and rapes occurred. These are anguishing events, and we are too close in time to not feel their blot on the collective self-image. They are fresh enough to color and contribute to a sense of existential crisis about Israel on its 60th anniversary. In each country's annals, including those of the United States, we must accept those facts we can't ignore, the dark actions that stain our history. Individuals may argue their significance, sometimes for generations to come. But we need only accept them as our past—we are not compelled to imbue them with any greater power in the present beyond accepting them and saying: How shall we go forward?

There will always be those, Jewish and not, who can only focus on Israel's wrongs as an indictment of all Israelis and Israel's right to exist. At the same time, there will always be those, Jewish and not, who will cite a double standard applied to Israel as a way to avoid confronting those wrongs in Israel's past and its present.

As each group gets more vocal, empowered by the Internet, blogs and a polarization that preaches opinion to its own fervent choir, it becomes increasingly difficult to stand up to the clatter and to voice a simple truth: That a true democracy thrives, regardless of the bad and regrettable actions of individuals in one regime's government (as is evidenced by what's going on right now in this country). That is the point of a democracy. A post-Zionist will continue to believe in Israel's dream of an open society, with truly democratic institutions and a democratic rule of law.

Herzl wrote his essay, "The Jewish State," in reaction to witnessing France's Dreyfus trial. Herzl felt that the only answer to the anti-Semitism he saw in Europe was to found a Jewish state. Today, we hear that anti-Semitism exists in Europe and elsewhere because of actions of the Jewish state (plus ca change....).

By some accounts, there are now more Jews living in Israel than in any single country in the world, yet anti-Semitism continues to flare up even in countries with little or no Jewish population.

How in this age of post-Zionism do we distinguish between criticism of Israel and its supporters (both Israeli and American), and criticism informed or motivated by anti-Semitism?

From my experience (and I have met quite a few Holocaust revisionists), more than anything, the issue boils down to the Gestalt, not the simple fact of criticism but the pattern, the language, the generalizations, the tone. Although that doesn't sound very precise (and I'm afraid it is not), let me refer you to someone who has done some serious research on the subject:

April Rosenblum, a Philadelphia-based progressive activist was troubled enough by her leftist friends not standing up to anti-Semitism that she produced a thirty-two page pamphlet, "The Past Didn't Go Anywhere." While critical of American and Israeli policies, the pamphlet explains in the language of the struggle how anti-Semitism weakens the cause of those committed to social action.

Rosenblum's is one response. But the point is that, for those imbued with the Gestalt of supporting and defending Israel, post-Zionism means finding a way to speak truth to Israel's faults as well as to those with anti-Semitic agendas.

As Israel turns sixty, post-Zionism is a love of Israel without borders, unafraid to accept truth and confident that a democratic Jewish state, despite its imperfections and failings, will continue to nourish our souls, and will one day fulfill its promise; and that as part of our covenant, we will continue to dream and work and support Israel, so that promise may come true in our lifetimes.

These words, which for years I've mumbled in Hebrew, without paying them any attention, seem strangely appropriate. They were written by Naftali Herz Imber in Zolochiv, Ukraine, in 1878. You may know them as the words to the Israeli national anthem, "Hatikvah":

As long as in the heart, within,

A soul of a Jew is yearning,

And to the edges of the East, forward,

An eye gazes toward Zion

Our hope is not yet lost,

The hope of two thousand years,

To be a free nation in our land,

The land of Zion and Jerusalem.

May 15, 2008

JAZZ: MADE IN NEW ORLEANS

I t's 2:00 a.m., and there's a crowd on St. Peter's Street in New Orleans' French Quarter; people are waiting to see the Stanton Moore Trio play Preservation Hall.

Midnight and early morning shows during Jazzfest are part of a new tradition initiated by Benjamin Jaffe, Preservation Hall's creative director, the man charged with safeguarding New Orleans' musical traditions, managing the Preservation Hall Jazz band and preserving Preservation Hall itself. The weekend I was there, the hall featured midnight performances by Tab Benoit, John Hammond Jr. and the Rebirth Brass Band.

Rebirth is the right word for New Orleans jazz.

Jaffe, who's in his late thirties and sports a serious Jewfro, is New Orleans born and raised. He comes to Preservation Hall both as a tuba and bass player who has toured with the band, and by birthright, as his parents, Allan and Sandra, launched what we've all come to know as Preservation Hall in 1961.

Allan Jaffe was born in Pottsville, Penn. (home of Yuengling beer), and graduated with a business degree from the Wharton School of the University of Pennsylvania, where he met his wife. His military service took him on his first trip to Louisiana and, after he finished serving, he and Sandra

found themselves back in New Orleans as part of an extend-
ed honeymoon—and they decided to stay.

In New Orleans, the Jaffes became part of a group interested
in preserving and promoting traditional New Orleans music.
At 726 St. Peter St., also in the French Quarter, Larry Boren-
stein, an art dealer, devoted part of his gallery, The Associated
Art Studios, to performances by these musicians. There was a
not-for-profit Society for the Preservation of Traditional Jazz
that had operated without much success. The Society dissolved
and, as was noted in a memo in the Hogan Jazz Archive at Tulane University, "beginning September 13, 1961, the work will
be continued on a for profit (or loss) basis, by Allan Jaffe and
his wife Sandy." Thus, the current Preservation Hall was born.

As Ben Jaffe explained when we talked in the courtyard
of Preservation Hall a few weeks ago, his parents were interested in the music, in preserving a tradition and a culture that
they were shocked to learn was in danger of disappearing, but
they also got involved out of a commitment to the Civil Rights
movement.

"To put things in perspective," Jaffe said, it was 1961, and
"The civil rights laws were not passed until 1964."

In 1961, some white New Orleans musicians, such as Pete
Fountain and Al Hirt, were finding popularity nationwide,
thanks to television programs such as the "Lawrence Welk
Show." However, the African American New Orleans artists,
many of whom were elderly, not only weren't getting on TV,
their music wasn't getting attention on radio, on records or in
New Orleans, for that matter.

Preservation Hall was a godsend for them. New Orleans musicians were eager for the gig—to play at Preservation Hall, Jaffe

called upon such legendary figures as trumpeters Kid Thomas Valentine, Kid Punch Miller, Kid Howard, De De Pierce, Percy Humphrey; clarinetist Willie Humphrey; and pianists such as Billie Pierce and Sweet Emma Barrett.

Given the pervasive segregation of the South at that time, white performers did not play with African American bands or tour with them—but Allan Jaffe did. He played tuba with the band and, as I learned from a publication of the Louisiana Historical society, he was said to be "the son of a mandolinist and music teacher and the grandson of a French horn player in a Russian Imperial band."

Preservation Hall's formula was simple and is followed to this day: No reservations, no food, just music in a small room. Shows began at 8 p.m. Each set lasted around thirty-five minutes, and tickets were priced low (they're now $10 a show, Wednesday through Sunday).

Part of Jaffe's plan to popularize New Orleans traditional music was to take the Preservation Hall Jazz Band on the road. In 1963, he took the band to Japan. Eventually it would play between 150 and 200 dates a year. Over the years, the Preservation Hall Jazz Band has played at such esteemed venues as New York's Lincoln Center, Symphony Hall in Boston and Royal Festival Hall in London, and has toured Israel and South America.

The band in its touring incarnation became the public face of traditional New Orleans jazz, but Preservation Hall itself became the soul.

The Jaffes became the custodians of an African American culture that they themselves became immersed in, as much as they became part of the city—and as much as they became part of the rich history of New Orleans' Jewish community.

Ben Jaffe told me that New Orleans was "a great city to grow up and be Jewish in." This was in part, he explained, "because we have so much respect for history and for culture and tradition, whether it's our own New Orleans traditions and cultures, whether it's African American, whether it's French or Spanish or our own Jewish traditions."

The Jewish community in New Orleans, Jaffe said, is "fairly tight-knit." He explained that he knew many of the families who formed the core of New Orleans' Jewish merchant class.

"The Rubenstein boys and I went to school together," he said, referencing the family whose department store, Rubenstein Brothers, is a New Orleans institution. "Their parents knew my parents from shul."

"When I think of New Orleans," Jaffe said, "I think of a city that embraces tradition and who we are, and celebrates it in ways completely unknown to the rest of the United States."

What is important to note about New Orleans, Jaffe said, is that "The Jewish community here has had a long and very healthy relationship with the African American community. It was the Jewish community that was the first to open its doors to the African American community, and open its store doors— clothing stores, furniture stores, appliance stores. There are a lot of African Americans that still only purchase from those furniture stores that originally sold only to African Americans.

"Rosenberg's on Tulane Avenue was the first furniture store that opened in an African American neighborhood, and to this day African Americans are loyal to that furniture store. Overwhelmingly," Jaffee said. Allan Jaffe died in 1987, at the age of fifty-one, of cancer. Ben was sixteen at the time. Sandra continued to run the Hall with her sister Risa, who took over the day-to-day operations.

Ben Jaffe's own involvement in Preservation Hall was not planned; it just evolved. He grew up in the Quarter, living a few blocks away from the hall. As a boy, he watched jazz funeral parades and Mardi Gras marches, and he hung out at Preservation Hall, where he heard many of New Orleans' greatest performers. Without any conscious effort, he absorbed it all. But he was more interested at that the time in reggae and rock 'n' roll. New Orleans jazz—that was his parents' music.

Looking back with 20/20 hindsight, Jaffe now says of hanging out at Preservation Hall: "That was my school."

He went to Oberlin College, known for its music program, and the day after Jaffe graduated in 1993, he flew to Paris and joined the Preservation Hall Jazz Band as its regular bass player. I asked Jaffe if he had to audition. He laughed, saying that it was a coincidence that the bass player had recently taken ill and stopped touring.

"The timing could not have been better," he said.

However, for him, "stepping into the band was a natural progression."

Jaffe played some 200 dates a year with the band and eventually took on managing the band and Preservation Hall, as well.

"At the time I simply felt motivated to keep Preservation Hall open and running," he said. "I never really had a mission statement or a business plan."

No plan could have prepared anyone for Hurricane Katrina in 2005, or its aftermath. Knowing that Preservation Hall, being in the French Quarter, was on high ground and that he could go there if needed, Jaffe remained in New Orleans. "We weathered the storm," he said, helping musicians get out of town—among them banjo and string bass virtuoso Narvin Kimball, then 95, whom Jaffe helped evacuate to Baton Rouge and whose banjos and photographs he helped remove from his home—luckily, because that's all that survived the storm. (Kimball died in South Carolina in 2006.)

"As everyone saw on television, it was a national embarrassment what took place here," Jaffe said.

He said the financial hardship was great and continues: "Our lives were shaken around like a snow globe."

Five out of seven members in the band lost their homes. They all suffered tremendous financial losses.

It's hard to appreciate, Jaffe explained, but people who had school-age children could not come back to New Orleans for at least a year—there were no schools and hospitals—and those with special-needs children could not get the services they needed. And once you've been living in another place for two years, it's hard to come back—who wants to be uprooted again?

"There are a million stories," Jaffe said, one for each of the evacuees, and each is different and filled with its own pain and difficult choices. "That's the hard part to understand."

That being said, Jaffe feels that the post-Katrina City of New Orleans has made an even greater commitment to New Orleans Jazz. The Hurricane Emergency Fund, which Jaffe co-founded, has evolved into "Renew Our Music," a grassroots community development organization. Jaffe released the box set *Made in New Orleans: The Hurricane Sessions,* which is a treasure trove and, in some ways, a collaboration between his late father and himself, incorporating early recordings and sessions interrupted by the Hurricane.

Preservation Hall has launched several education and outreach programs for schools and children. Jaffe has also been able to work on several projects with The Jazz and Heritage Foundation and the State of Louisiana, including launching SYNC UP, cutting-edge online technology that allows music supervisors to search for New Orleans musicians and music to use or license for film and television.

More than forty-five years after his parents established Preservation Hall, Jaffe feels New Orleans' music is rich in history and well stocked with new generations of artists filled with a love of traditional New Orleans Jazz (which is refreshed and reinvented each time it's played).

Jaffe also has established a fairly exhaustive database of New Orleans musicians: "I can't tell you the last time I went to a show [in New Orleans] and saw a musician and didn't know who they were."

He cites jazz trumpeter Mark Braud, grandson of trumpeter John "Pickett" Brunious Sr., and nephew of Preservation Hall's John Brunious Jr., as being a fourth-generation jazz artist.

"Find me a fourth-generation anything, anywhere," Jaffe said.

So, next time you head down to New Orleans, stop in at Preservation Hall. Chances are you'll find Ben Jaffe there, a fourth-generation musician who's the second generation to run the hall.

Tell him Tommywood sent you. That and ten dollars will get you a seat to hear America's indigenous art form, a living tradition that is the heart and soul of a city, the music that made New Orleans.

May 29, 2008

ALSO BY TOM TEICHOLZ

Greetings from Tommywood, (Volume One).Pondwood Press, 2015.

Son of Tommywood, (Volume Two). Pondwood Press, 2015.

Tommywood Jr., Jr.: The Gospel According to Tommywood (Volume Four). Pondwood Press, 2015.

Fast Furious Tommywood (Volume Five). Pondwood Press, 2015.

Close Encounters of the Tommywood Kind (Volume Six). Pondwood Press, 2015.

Wilshire Boulevard Temple and the Warner Murals: Celebrating 150 Years by Tom Teicholz, Oro Editions, San Francisco, CA 2014.

The Jewish Role in American Life, Casden Insitute Annual Study, Volume 1, by Barry Glassner, Hillary Lachner, and Tom Teicholz, USC / Casden Institute, Los Angeles, CA, 2008.

Like No Other Store: Bloomingdale's and the Revolution in American Marketing by Marvin Traub and Tom Teicholz, Times Books/Random House, New York, New York, 1993.

The Trial of Ivan The Terrible: State of Israel vs. John Demjanjuk by Tom Teicholz, St.Martin's Press, New York, New York, 1990.

Conversations with Jerzy Kosinski, edited and with an introduction by Tom Teicholz, University Press of Mississippi, Jackson, Mississippi, 1993.

Conversations with S. J. Perelman, edited and with an introduction by Tom Teicholz, University Press of Mississippi, Jackson, Mississippi, 1995.

Other books and anthologies containing Tom Teicholz's work:

Encyclopedia Judaica, Second Edition. Tom Teicholz, American Film
and TV editor., 2006.
Conversations with Isaac Bashevis Singer, University Press of Mississippi,
Jackson, Mississippi, 1992.
Writers at Work, Volume 8, The Paris Review Interviews, Viking/Pen-
guin, New York, 1988.

ACKNOWLEDGEMENTS

I want to thank the contributors to The TOMMYWOOD Collection IndieGogo campaign for their support and generosity which made publication possible, most notably my tzadiks, hoochems and benefactors: Sandy Climan, Bracken Darrell, Lawrence Schoen, Toni and John Schulman, Bob & Cori Davenport, Peter Graham and Heidi Drymer, Ken & Teri Hertz, Wally & Helen Weiss, Dede Arnholz, Chuck Leavitt, Sharon Nazarian, Chris Pilkington, Stacy and Massimo Pinello, Robert & Edie Parker, Annie Schichili, and Richard Wolloch.

There is more to a book than just writing its content. You need talented people to successfully prepare it for publication. The reason this book looks so terrific is because of designer Devin Tanchum and the very talented folks at Rare Bird Lit, notably my book guru Tyson Cornell and his excellent associates Alice Elmer and Violet Sarosi, as well as Winona Leon (who did the design work for my IndieGogo Campaign). I also want to thank John Vaskis and John Trigonis at IndieGogo for teaching me so much about crowdfunding and helping make this book possible.

ABOUT THE AUTHOR

Tom Teicholz is an award-winning journalist, producer, and content consultant who has created print, video, and social media content for Intel, Logitech, The Museum of Tolerance, and The Milken Family Foundation as well as for several not-for-profits and private clients. His work has appeared in *The New York Times* Sunday magazine, *The Los Angeles Review of Books*, *The Los Angeles Times* Op-Ed page, Newsweek.com, *The Paris Review*, *The New Yorker's* 'Talk of the Town', *Narrative Magazine*, Forbes.com and the *Huffington Post*. He lives with his wife and daughter in Santa Monica, CA.

CPSIA information can be obtained
at www.ICGtesting.com
Printed in the USA
FSOW02n1733160615
7982FS